Radio Times

AROUND BRITAIN GUIDE

London & the South East

Researched and edited by

JAMES TINDALL

NETWORK BOOKS

RADIO TIMES AROUND BRITAIN GUIDE
London & the South East

First published in Great Britain
by Network Books in 1993

Network Books is an imprint of BBC Enterprises Ltd.,
Woodlands, 80 Wood Lane, London W12 0TT

Designed by Paul Simpson
Produced by Lovell Johns Ltd. of Oxford and St. Asaph.

Printed in Great Britain by Victoria Litho, Ltd. London.

A catalogue record for this book is available from the British Library

ISBN 0-563-36951-5

CONTENTS

Welcome to the **RADIO TIMES AROUND BRITAIN GUIDES**. Each guide covers one specific region of the country.

This new series was conceived to fill two needs.

First, to give the discerning TV viewer and radio listener an effective guide to the major attractions within each region, including a brief insight into why they are worth visiting and information on when they may be visited. This section is sub-divided into a number of different types of attractions including a special listing of attractions that are specifically designed for the whole family.

Second, to provide an overview of the companies responsible for broadcasting within each region and the contribution they make nationally as well as on a regional basis. This section of broadcast information also includes brief guides to some of the most popular programmes generated there, a guide to the major televised sporting venues and a personal view of the region by a local media personality.

The guides are illustrated with a wide range of photographs, most of which were supplied by the individual attractions and I am most grateful for the assistance these establishments and their owners and staff have given us.

The TV stills and other broadcast photographs were provided by the television and radio companies and, again, I am very grateful for the assistance the various press offices have given us during the research on this guide.

As these are the first editions of the **RADIO TIMES AROUND BRITAIN GUIDES** we may well have missed some attractions that you feel should be included. We have travelled each region and trawled all the available information from the local Tourist Information Centres but if you feel that there is something else we should include please write via Network Books and we will evaluate your suggestion with a view to including it in the next edition.

I hope that you find this guide useful and enjoyable.

London & the South East

A background to ....

London and the South East is unique in containing both the nation's capital city and some very pleasant countryside. The region covers the Greater London area and the counties of Kent, Surrey and Sussex.

The best of the region's landscape can be found in the North and South Downs and the Weald.

The region's vast importance in royal, court, military, religious and commercial matters can be clearly gauged by flicking through the listings sections. It is very difficult anywhere within the region to find yourself more than 20 miles away from a site of major historic importance and in central London it is impossible to escape them.

London's famous Tower Bridge

However, the delights of *London and the South East* are not purely historic nor just found in great houses and museums. It contains nationally important relics from Roman times onwards but is still a thriving, lively region in which tens of millions of people live and work.

The working attractions of the region include modern engineering masterpieces such as **Eurotunnel** and the **Thames Barrier** but there are also working mills, commercial woods and some spectacular working steam railways.

What will probably come as a surprise to many people are the number of successful commercial vineyards in the region.

There is also a great deal of effort expended on wildlife and ecology and particularly on protecting and breeding endangered species. The world's oldest public zoo, **London Zoo**, is in the middle of a process of change to reflect these developments whilst centres such as **John Aspinall's** at **Howletts** and **Port Lympne** are fine examples of what can be achieved.

Additionally, almost nowhere in the country is as well provided with entertainment centres for days out. In **Chessington World of Adventures** and **Thorpe Park** the region has two of the country's finest theme parks but there are other significant theme and fun parks scattered throughout the region.

The Thames Barrier, a modern engineering masterpiece

The Flying Fish is an exciting family roller coaster ride at Thorpe Park

Television in the region is provided by the BBC from its headquarters at the Television Centre in White City. For ITV, from 1st January 1993, by Carlton TV and LWT for the Greater London area and by Meridian for the south of the region. Channel 4's nationwide coverage comes from London.

BBC Television was born at Alexandra Palace in North London in 1936 but was "switched off" for the duration of World War Two and did not resume broadcasting until 1946. Although the BBC had broadcast a number of major events including the 1948 Olympics from Wembley it was the present Queen's Coronation in 1953 that really generated the first mass interest in the new medium by the general British public. BBC Television expanded over the years and used a number of sites until, in 1960, the purpose built Television Centre in White City was opened.
Although the major regional centres such as Pebble Mill in Birmingham and New Broadcasting House in Manchester produce a significant number of network programmes the vast majority of the BBC's huge annual production is generated from Television Centre.

The Eurotunnel
Exhibition Centre

The Runaway Minetrain
at Chessington
World of Adventures

London was also the first area of the country to receive independent television. The service started on 22nd September 1955 and the original franchise holders were Associated-Rediffusion [weekdays] and ATV [weekends]. In 1968 these two companies were replaced by Thames TV and London Weekend Television, in 1993 LWT retained its franchise but Thames lost out to newcomer Carlton TV. Thames TV became a TV production company and still produces for the network major series including **"Minder"** and **"The Bill"**.

Kristen Scott Thomas stars as Anna in"Body & Soul"

Carlton are a publisher company rather than a producer, they commission new projects or buy completed projects from production companies rather than generating them in-house. They are based in central London and their current output includes **"Body and Soul"**, **"Fantastic Facts"**, **"Michael Ball"** and **"Storyline"**.

"In the Company of Wolves"

LWT are one of the major, established ITV companies and have their headquarters in the London Television Centre on the South Bank of the Thames. Their current output includes **"Agatha Christie's Poirot"**, **"Aspel and Company"**, **"Barrymore"**, **"Blind Date"**, **"Forever Green"**, **"Hale and Pace"**, **"Sam Saturday"** and **"The South Bank Show"**.

"Aspel and Company"

Meridian are also ITV newcomers and are publishers rather than producers. They have Central London offices and a Television Centre in Maidstone in Kent as well as other facilities outside the *London and the South East* region. Their recent and current output includes **"Catchphrase"**, **"Harnessing Peacocks"**, **"In The Company Of Wolves"** and **"Over The Rainbow"**.

Michael Barrymore and "friend"

Channel 4 is also a publisher rather than a producer. It was the first publisher TV company in the country and was used as a model for many of the companies in the 1993 franchise round. Its headquarters are in Charlotte Street in central London and the entire national output of the station is generated from there.

London is also the headquarters for BBC Radio, at Broadcasting House in Portland Place, the historic home of the service and Lord Reith's power base. It still generates the vast majority of the national radio network's output.

There are BBC local radio stations covering the entire region including GLR which covers Greater London.

The major independent radio stations in the region include Capital Radio and LBC, both of which cover Greater London, Invicta Radio in Kent, Radio Mercury in Surrey and Southern Sound in Sussex.

"Over the Rainbow"

"Agatha Christie's Poirot"

"Surprise Surprise" with Cilla Black

Why I love London & the South East

David Jason

David Jason is one of the most successful actors in Britain. After a successful background on the stage his first major TV role was starring with Ronnie Barker in Open All Hours in 1975. The blockbusting Only Fools and Horses started in 1981 and Jason's Del Boy became one of the nation's favourite characters. This was followed in 1986 by Porterhouse Blue and 1988 saw the first Bit Of A Do. A decision to televise H.E. Bates' stories of life in rural Kent led to Jason being cast as Pa Larkin and the first episode of The Darling Buds of May was shown in 1990. It was an immensely popular hit and, once again, David Jason had created an unbeatable character.

So why does he love London and the South East.

It's a unique area of the country. You have the hustle, bustle and excitement of the city, be it Del Boy's Peckham or the swish, up-market West End and yet if you drive 30 miles you can be in the heart of Wealden countryside so

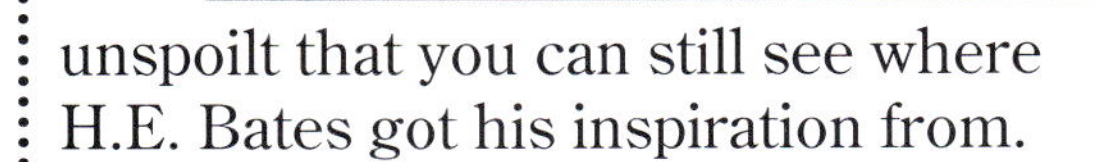

unspoilt that you can still see where H.E. Bates got his inspiration from.

It's an area that literally tingles with history, that's been fought over by great, proud people for thousands of years and that has been the great cornerstone of England ever since William landed at Hastings.

But again, you don't have to be in London to see it, throughout the area you can find examples, not just castles and palaces, although they're impressive enough, but all the other great houses and gardens. People have lived, loved and flourished in the area for thousands of years and the people who live here now are their successors.

Its not just history and tradition though, it's also great fun. Everyone enjoys a good day out, look at some of the Larkin family outings. If you cannot find a place around here to have fun then you must be dead. For a real treat for all the family we've got some really marvellous theme parks and the one you love is bound to hang on to you tightly whilst you're on the white knuckle rides!

A day out doesn't have to be hectic though. There are some wonderful museums around the area. Some of them include replicas of how our corner shops used to look in Victorian times and for the little boy in all of us there are some great steam trains.

Or if you fancy a great English tradition why not go for a day at the seaside, a walk along the prom, fun on the pier, "kiss me quick" hats and fish and chips and its only just over an hour on the train from South East London to Brighton, and that's only one of dozens of seaside resorts in the area.

Speaking of fish and chips leads us on naturally to food and how can you go wrong in London and the South East, you must be able to get every type of food in the world somewhere in the area. If you want good home cooking, ranging from farmhouse food that Ma Larkin would be proud of to cream teas in the garden then you'll find that dozens of the attractions in the area also have a tea room or cafe and you can always be guaranteed a warm welcome.

That's it really, whatever you want to do and see, from high culture to letting your hair down, whether you're a single man about town or a country loving man with a large family, you'll find it, in London and the South East.

David Jason as Pa Larkin

TV SCENES *of London life*

Outsiders often divide London into distinct and separate units and the perceived characteristics and lifestyles of people within the different units are often a result of TV series rather than real life. Classic examples are the caricatured views of three areas of London as portrayed on TV.
Another, equally prevalent view of London Life is devised by the London policeman as he has been depicted over the decades.

West London

West London stretches from exclusive Kensington to Hammersmith, Chiswick, Ealing and beyond and includes some of the finest homes and shopping in London. However, because of two exceptionally successful TV series when most people think of West London they immediately think of Shepherds Bush.

"Steptoe and Son", the story of the Bush's most famous rag and bone men was launched by the BBC in 1962. Harry H. Corbett played Harold, the son, and Wilfred Brambell played Steptoe. They dodged, dived and dealt to earn a living from their trade with Harold always trying to improve himself and Steptoe always bringing him crashing back to the ground and reality. Only 40 episodes were ever made but the series was both popular with viewers and adored by critics. It created a view of West London life, living by your wits somewhere in the ill-defined zone between crooked and straight, which was to be consolidated in the early 1980s by one of the most successful TV series ever.

"Minder" was launched on ITV at the end of 1979 with George Cole playing Arthur Daley the West London car dealer and would-be businessman who sometimes sailed so close to the wind that he needed ex-boxer Terry McCann, played by Dennis Waterman, as his minder. The car lot, the

Winchester Club and many of the series' other locations were scattered around Shepherds Bush, Brook Green and Acton. The storylines and the situations Daley got himself into definitely confirmed that if you lived in West London you needed a sharp brain, fast feet ... and a good minder.

East London

If West London life was caricatured by Steptoe and Daley then life in the East End of London has been defined by a number of memorable TV series over the last thirty years. Of all of the TV series based in the East End three probably had the greatest impact on the viewing public's perception of the area.

The first was **"The Larkins"**, launched by ITV in 1959 it starred David Kossoff and Peggy Mount as Alf and Ada, the patriach and matriach of a typical cockney family. It ran until 1964 and was one of the funniest and most popular TV series ever produced.

In 1966 the East End inheritors of the mantle of the Larkins and Alf were the Garnetts and Alf as the BBC launched **"Till Death Us Do Part"**. Warren Mitchell was superb as Alf, a man devoted to the Queen, Winston Churchill and West Ham Football Club and vehemently opposed to anything new or revolutionary. Dandy Nicholls played his long suffering wife Else and Una Stubbs and Anthony Booth made up the rest of the Garnett family.

Until 1985 most programmes based in East London were comedies exploiting the natural humour of Cockneys and their lifestyle. There had been experiments in more serious drama, particularly during the two year run of the series **"Market at Honey Lane"**. 1985 however saw the launch of the series that was to personify East London life for most viewers as thoroughly as **"Coronation Street"** personifies Northern life. In February that year BBC launched the long awaited soap **"EastEnders"**. As with most new soaps it faced a tough baptism but it survived and eight years later its twice weekly portrait of life in Albert Square with gritty storylines and a great deal of social realism attracts an average audience per episode of between 18 and 20 million and it often takes the Number One spot in the national ratings.

Wilfrid Brambell as Albert Steptoe and Harry H. Corbett as his son Harold

Ross Kemp as Grant Michell and Letitia Dean as his wife Sharon in "EastEnders"

South East London

Very few television series have been based in South East London but one spectacular gem makes up for the lack of other programmes. Nelson Mandela House in Peckham became famous as the home of Del Boy and Rodney, the Trotters, in BBC's **"Only Fools And Horses"**. First shown in 1981 it became one of the TV hits of the 1980s. Del Boy's character and lifestyle strikes interesting parallels with his contemporary West London "rival" **Arthur Daley**, so maybe the only way to succeed in **"TV London"** is by a combination of wits and staying one jump ahead of the law. In any case **"Only Fools And Horses"** attracted up to 16 million viewers per episode in the late 1980s.

"Only Fools and Horses" starring David Jason as "Del Boy", Nicholas Lyndhurst as "Rodney" and Buster Merryfield as "Uncle Albert"

London Police series

Over the decades many television series have been built around the work of the police and particularly, presumably because of their distinctive role as the capital's guardians, the Metropolitan Police. This line of television drama can be traced continuously from the cosy 1950s world of "Dixon of Dock Green" to the hard storylines of "The Bill" in the 1990s.

Dixon was the first major police series, it was launched by the BBC in 1955 and ran for 21 years. It was based in London's Docklands and portrayed them as they were before the closure of the docks, degeneration of the area and "regeneration" with office blocks and incoming yuppies. **Reg Dixon's** manor was very much a village with **Jack Warner** playing the title role as a kind of village bobby, even the bad guys were never too bad and both they and the locals treated **Dixon** and his colleagues with respect.

The BBC launched a second police series later on in 1955. It had two particular features which TV stations would return to time and again over the years; first, it was based around the work of **Scotland Yard** and; second, it was a series of fictionalised accounts of true stories. It was called **"Fabian of Scotland Yard"**.

ITV was launched in September 1955 and one of its first locally produced series was also based at Scotland Yard, **"Colonel March of Scotland Yard"** was, for its time, an unusual and inventive series. **Boris Karloff** played **Colonel March**, the officer in charge of the Yard's Queer Complaints Department, a specialist unit involved in solving cases that had baffled everyone else.

One of the most memorable London police series was launched by ITV in 1957 and ran for ten years although it changed its name three times in the first two years. It began as a series called **"Murder Bag"**, became **"Crime Sheet"** and, in September 1959, settled on the name **"No Hiding Place"**. Over the next eight years it became one of the most popular series on TV and made **Chief Detective Superintendent Lockhart** and actor **Raymond Francis** household names.

Euston Films, part of Thames TV, created two successful drama series out of the work of real life specialist departments within Scotland Yard. The first, launched in 1969, was **"Special Branch"** and developed fictional storylines around the roles of Special Branch in surveillance, security and counter espionage, it starred **Patrick Mower** and **George Sewell** and ran until the mid 1970s. Euston Films' second series was launched in January 1975, was based on the work of Scotland Yard's famous Flying Squad and became the TV police series of the 1970s. It was called **"The Sweeney"**, starred **John Thaw** and **Dennis Waterman** as all-action hard men **Regan and Carter** and ran for three years.

Jack Warner as Sgt. Dixon in "Dixon of Dock Green"

In contrast to the Yard-based police series of the 1970s the first few years of the 1980s saw the arrival of three London police series based in "ordinary" police stations, two of them with unusual leading characters. In 1980 ITV launched **"The Gentle Touch"**, the first series to have a woman in the leading role, **Jill Gascoigne** played **Inspector Maggie Forbes**. A year later the BBC launched **"The Chinese Detective"** with **David Yip** playing **Johnny Ho**.

The third series started in 1983 as a pilot programme called **"Woodentop"**, the pilot was well received and was turned into a series. The series gained in popularity over the years and now broadcasts three half an hour episodes each week. It is the most popular regular weekly non-soap on TV with each episode attracting between 12 and 15 million viewers. Telling the story of the day-to-day working lives and tensions of the detectives and uniformed officers at **Sun Hill Police Station** it is **"The Bill"**.

"The Bill"

MAJOR TELEVISED SPORTING VENUES

in London & the South East

Athletics

Many venues in the South East, particularly London, have hosted athletic events including Wembley, venue of the last Olympic Games to be hosted by this country. The most prestigious venue for athletics is the Crystal Palace National Sports Centre.

Crystal Palace National Sports Centre

Crystal Palace Park, London SE26
☎ 081 778 0131

The Crystal Palace complex houses facilities for a very wide range of sporting activities including swimming and diving, squash, gymnastics, hockey, tennis and badminton. The focal point of the complex is the floodlit athletics stadium, the home of many major athletics meetings including the TSB Games. In September 1993 it will host the Athletics Grand Prix Final, the first time the final has taken place in Britain.

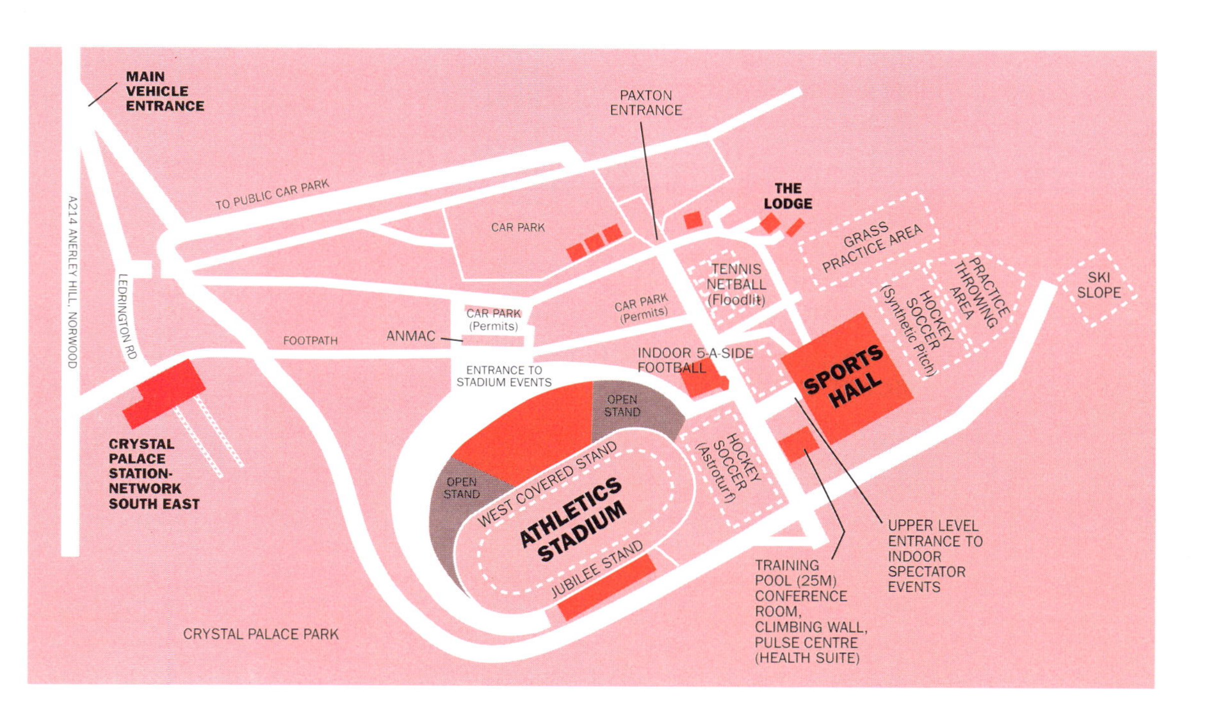

Rugby Union

Many of the most famous rugby union clubs in the country have their grounds in *London and the South East* and it is also the home of the heart of rugby union, Twickenham.

Twickenham

Twickenham, Middlesex
☎ 081 892 8161

The Rugby Football Union was formed in 1871 to establish the rules of the game and select an England team to play other nations. Many home and away internationals where organised but England had no official "home ground" until 1907 when the RFU bought a 10 acre market garden in Twickenham and began converting it into a stadium. The original layout combined stand seats with open terracing and had a capacity of 30,000. Over the last 20 years the RFU has spent millions of pounds developing Twickenham into one of the world's great sports stadiums, the new South Stand was opened in 1981 and the new North Stand in 1991 and these increased the capacity to 60,000. Work is still underway at the ground and the RFU are close to fulfilling their ambition of creating a luxurious 75,000 capacity all-seater stadium. It is the venue for all England's home games as well as televised classics such as The Varsity Match and the Middlesex Sevens and was the venue for the 1991 World Cup Final. The RFU also run a rugby museum at Twickenham and a shop.

Tennis

Tennis is played throughout *London and the South East* with notable tournaments being played at Eastbourne and at London's Queen's Club. The highlight of Britain's tennis year for hundreds of thousands of paying spectators and millions of television viewers is the annual Wimbledon Championships.

All England Lawn Tennis and Croquet Club

Church Road, Wimbledon, London SW19
⊖ Southfields
☎ 081 946 6497

The All England Lawn Tennis and Croquet Club was founded on 23rd July 1868 as the All England Croquet Club and acquired a ground in Worple Road, Wimbledon. The club started playing tennis in 1875 and in 1877 the words "and Lawn Tennis" were added to the club's name and it took over the administration of the game from the club that had previously run tennis, the Marylebone Cricket Club. The club moved to a new 13 1/2 acre site in Church Road, Wimbledon in 1922 and has been there ever since. It was televised for the first time in 1937 but remained an "amateurs-only" competition until 1968 when the first open championship was held. It is one of the four world Grand Slam Events, the only one still played on grass and is regarded worldwide as the home of tennis. The Centre Court has a capacity of just over 13,000 and in 1991 the total attendance over the fortnight was 378,411. The prizes make interesting reading. In 1877 the winning man received a gold prize valued at 12 guineas. In 1884, the first year of the Ladies' Singles, the winner received a silver flower basket valued at 20 guineas. From 1968 onwards, with the Championship an open event, prize money was awarded. In 1968 the Gentlemen's Singles Champion received £2,000 and the Ladies' Singles Champion £750. By 1991 these figures had risen to £240,000 and £216,000 respectively. All of Wimbledon's energies are concentrated on planning, managing and running the fortnight at the end of June and start of July, there are sometimes other events at Wimbledon but the last one was the Davies Cup in 1986. There is a Lawn Tennis Museum at the ground that is open to the public every day except for on Mondays and during the Championship.

The planned new look Wimbledon Tennis Complex for the 21st century

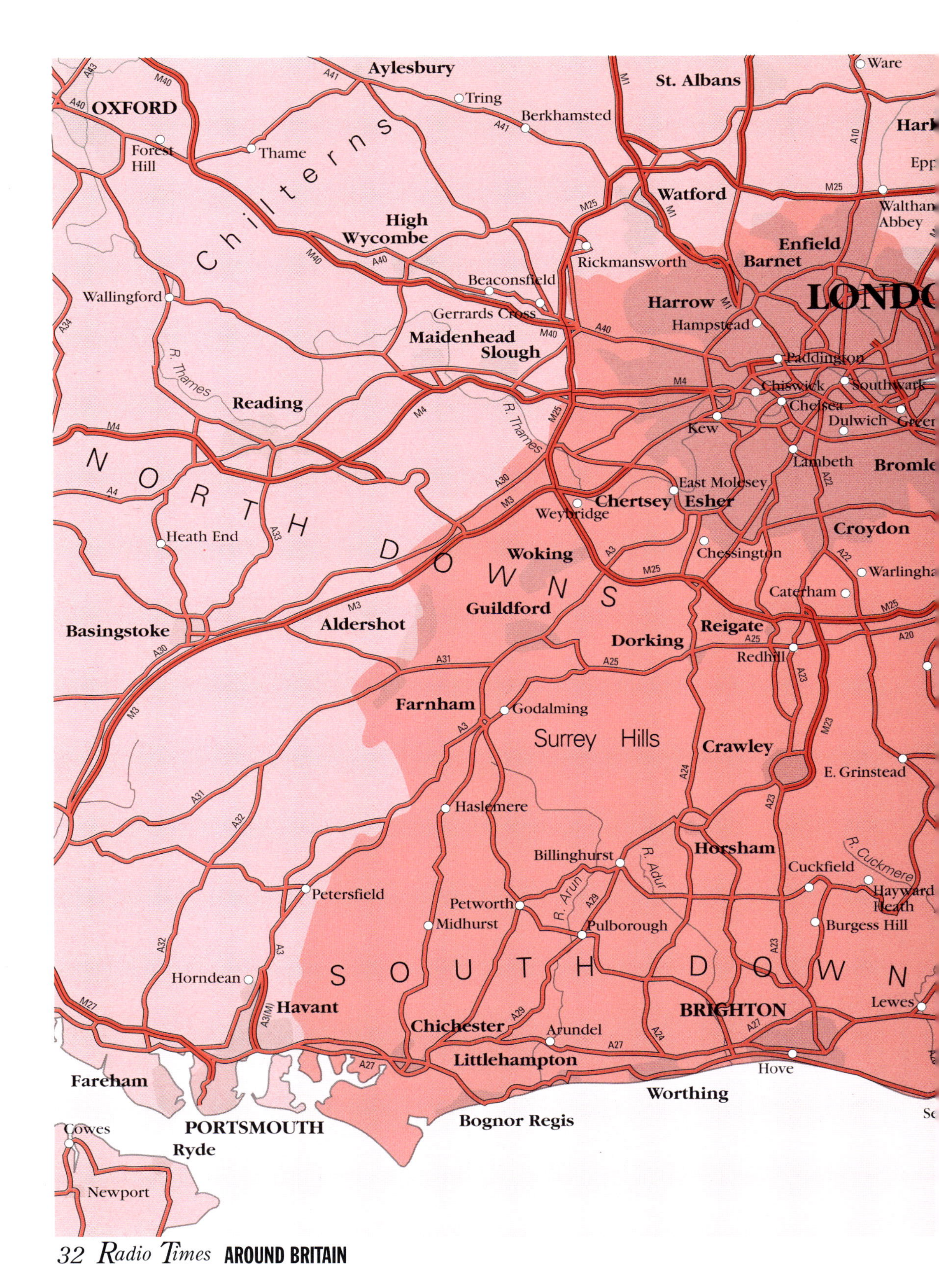

Aylesbury
St. Albans
Ware
OXFORD
Tring
Berkhamsted
Forest Hill
Thame
Chilterns
Watford
Waltham Abbey
High Wycombe
Rickmansworth
Enfield
Barnet
Wallingford
Beaconsfield
Harrow
Gerrards Cross
Hampstead
Maidenhead
Slough
R. Thames
Paddington
Chiswick
Southwark
Reading
Chelsea
Dulwich
Kew
NORTH DOWNS
Lambeth
East Molesey
Chertsey
Esher
Weybridge
Heath End
Croydon
Woking
Chessington
Caterham
Guildford
Basingstoke
Aldershot
Reigate
Dorking
Redhill
Farnham
Godalming
Surrey Hills
Crawley
E. Grinstead
Haslemere
Horsham
Billinghurst
R. Adur
R. Cuckmere
Cuckfield
Hayward Heath
Petersfield
Petworth
R. Arun
Midhurst
Pulborough
Burgess Hill
SOUTH DOWN
Horndean
Lewes
Havant
BRIGHTON
Chichester
Arundel
Littlehampton
Hove
Fareham
Worthing
Cowes
PORTSMOUTH
Bognor Regis
Ryde
Newport

Maldon
R. Blackwater
W. Mersea
Clacton-On-Sea
Chelmsford
Witham
NORTH SEA
Brentwood
Burnham-On-Crouch
Basildon
Southend-On-Sea
Tilbury
Sheerness
Gravesend
Margate
Herne Bay
Birchington
Gillingham
Rochester
Chatham
Sittingbourne
Herne
Whitstable
Faversham
Ramsgate
R. Stour
Eynsford
NORTH DOWNS
Canterbury
Sandwich
Sevenoaks
Maidstone
R. Medway
Deal
Tonbridge
Walmer
Paddock Wood
Brenchley
Headcorn
Ashford
Staplehurst
Dover
Goudhurst
Cranbrook
Hythe
Folkestone
Frant
Lamberhurst
Tenterden
Rolvenden
Bewl Water
R. Rother
Burwash
New Romney
Heathfield
Robertsbridge
Rye
Lydd
High Weald
Battle
Dungeness
STRAIT OF DOVER
Hailsham
Hastings
Pevensey
Bexhill
Eastbourne
30 Kilometres
19 Miles

What to see in London & the South East........

1

1. London Dungeon
2. Thorpe Park
3. Arundel Castle
4. Blean Bird Park
5. London Toy and Model Museum

2

3

4

5

What to see in *London and the South East*

HOW TO USE THIS SECTION

The attractions are listed under the following categories:

PARKS & GARDENS
ANTIQUITIES
HISTORIC BUILDINGS
RELIGIOUS BUILDINGS
MUSEUMS & ART GALLERIES
WORKING ATTRACTIONS
STEAM RAILWAYS
FOOD & DRINK
WILDLIFE
THE REGION AT PLAY

When an attraction is of interest in more than one category, particularly for example Historic Buildings many of which also have interesting Parks and Gardens, then other entries for the attraction are cross-referenced at the end of the attraction's listing.

For each attraction the following information is provided:

HISTORIC BUILDINGS

Cabinet War Rooms
King Charles Street, London SW1
⊖ Westminster

NAME OF ATTRACTION
NEAREST TOWN OR VILLAGE or AREA OF CITY
these are not directional guides and should be used in conjunction with a good road atlas or street plan, to enable you to find the attractions in London we have also listed the nearest London Underground "tube" station

The Imperial War Museum administers this suite of 21 underground rooms. They were used by Sir Winston Churchill, his Cabinet and armed services chiefs as the protected nerve centre from which they conducted World War Two and were in continuous use from 1939 until 1945. They have been restored to their appearance during those years and include the Cabinet Room, Transatlantic Telephone Room, Map Room and the Prime Minister's Sitting and Bedroom.

BRIEF DESCRIPTION OF THE ATTRACTION
with information on its greatest points of interest and notes on shops and refreshment facilities

Open every day except for over the Christmas period and New Years Day.

OPENING PERIODS
when the attraction is open during the year, actual hours of opening should be confirmed by a telephone call to the attraction, please note that even when an attraction describes itself as "Open All Year" it might well close over the Christmas Period

☎ 071 930 6961

TELEPHONE NUMBER
to enable you to contact the attraction direct in order to check for special events or confirm its suitability for disabled people, large parties, etc. The majority of attractions charge admission and the current prices can be confirmed by telephoning the attraction

Bedgebury National Pinetum

Near Goudhurst, Kent

Some of the trees in Bedgebury's 150 acres were planted more than a century ago whilst the area was a private estate but most of the present layout has been created since 1924 when it became a Forestry Commission area. There are many rare specimens of conifers in the collection and these are visible from the waymarked trails. There is a visitor centre and a picnic site.

Open every day except Christmas Day.

☎ 0580 211044

PARKS & GARDENS

Borde Hill Garden

Borde Hill, near Haywards Heath, West Sussex

The garden features both formal gardens with rare plants and parkland and woodland estates. It has been planted and cared for over the last one hundred years. It is famous for its camellias and rhododendrons but also contains many unusually species including plants from Burma and China. There are walks through the woodlands. There is a children's adventure playground, a gift shop and a plant centre. There are also restaurants and picnic sites.

Open every day between April and early October and on Sundays in March and October.

☎ 0444 450326

Borde Hill Garden features both formal gardens with rare plants and parkland and woodland estates

PARKS & GARDENS

Brickwall Gardens
Northiam, near Rye, East Sussex

The house at the centre of the garden is 17th century Jacobean. The formal gardens are splendid. They have a grand terracotta entrance gate and are divided by 17th century walls and Yew hedges. The gardens include a sunken topiary garden, an arboretum, an unusual chess garden and an early 18th century bowling alley. There is a picnic area in the grounds and a shop.

Open between April and the end of September on Saturdays and Bank Holiday Mondays only.

☎ 0797 223329

Chilham Castle Gardens
Chilham, near Canterbury, Kent

The Jacobean mansion at Chilham Castle was built in 1616 by Sir Dudley Digges within the foundations of a 12th century castle of which only the Keep remains. The castle is surrounded by a 250 acre deer park that was created in the 18th century by James Colebrooke. The formal gardens were created by John Tradescant in the 17th century and make use of terraces and topiary. They contain the King Holm Oak, an evergreen oak on the upper lawn that was planted in 1616 to mark the completion of the new mansion and is still growing. The Rose Garden contains some mulberry trees grown from the original stock that provided cuttings for the trees planted on the USA's Mulberry Island in the 17th century. The large lake was laid out by Charles Stuart Hardy in the 19th century and the adjoining Rock Garden was created in the 1930s by Sir Edmund Davies. Chilham Castle also includes a Raptor Centre for birds of prey and a children's petland. There is a gift shop and a tea room and picnic site. There are special events at weekends throughout the Summer.

Open every day between April and mid October.

☎ 0227 730319

SEE ALSO *WILDLIFE*

Claremont Landscape Garden
Esher, Surrey

Claremont is regarded by many as the finest and is certainly the earliest natural English landscape garden surviving in this country and was the work of an outstanding collaboration of talents. The garden was commissioned by Thomas Pelham in 1711 and was created by Charles Bridgeman and Sir John Vanbrugh. They finished in 1726 and in 1727 it was described it as "the noblest garden in Europe". In later years the garden was extended and further developed by both William Kent and Capability Brown but both worked within Bridgeman's overall concept. The major features include the lake, Bridgeman's spectacular turf amphitheatre and the grotto. The garden is maintained by the National Trust. It hosts a fete every July and there is a shop and a tea room.

Open every day except for Mondays between November and the end of March and Christmas Day and New Years Day.

☎ 0372 469930

The Jacobean mansion at Chilham Castle was built in 1616 by Sir Dudley Digges

Denmans Garden
Fontwell, near Arundel, West Sussex

Denmans features a variety of garden styles including a walled garden featuring roses and herbs, a gravel garden of grasses and bamboos and a water garden. There are also glasshouses containing rare and delicate plants and a wild garden. There is a school of garden design which holds regular one-day courses, a plant centre and craft shop and a tea shop.

Open every day between March and Christmas Eve.

☎ 0243 542808

Emmetts
Ide Hill, near Sevenoaks, Kent

A 5 acre hilltop garden looked after by the National Trust. It contains many fine specimens of trees and shrubs and is famous for its Spring and Autumn colours. Some of the formal gardens are in the process of restoration and the Rock Garden and Rose Garden have been restored and reopened. There is a tea room.

Open every day from April to the end of October except Tuesdays and non-Bank Holiday Mondays.

☎ 0892 890651

PARKS & GARDENS

Great Dixter House and Gardens

Northiam, near Rye, East Sussex

Great Dixter House is a timber-framed manor house built in the 15th century and restored and extended at the start of this century by Sir Edwin Lutyens. It houses a collection of antique furniture. Lutyens, working with Gertrude Jekyll, also designed and laid out the delightful gardens. The main features of these include a rose garden, a sunken garden and a topiary garden. The herbaceous borders are also fine. There is a shop selling plants and gifts.

The house and gardens are open in the afternoons between April and the middle of October excluding non-Bank Holiday Mondays; additionally, the gardens are open all day over the Whitsun Bank Holiday Sunday and Monday, all day every Sunday in July and August and all day on the Late Summer Bank Holiday Monday.

☎ 0797 253160

SEE ALSO *HISTORIC BUILDINGS*

Hampton Court Palace

East Molesey, Surrey

Hampton Court Palace was built by Cardinal Wolsey in 1514 and "given" to Henry VIII in 1529. The original

PARKS & GARDENS

Tudor features were sympathetically extended by Sir Christopher Wren. The garden and grounds include formal gardens, water gardens, an Orangery and a Wilderness. Within the grounds near the Palace is the famous Hampton Court Maze, created in 1690. Another famous feature of the gardens is the Great Vine, planted in 1768 it is the largest in England and has branches more than 110 feet long and produces more than 700lbs of black grapes every year. There is a gift shop, a tea room and picnic spots.

Open every day.

☎ 081 977 8441

SEE ALSO *HISTORIC BUILDINGS*

Headcorn Flower Centre and Vineyard

Headcorn, Kent

The centre has a number of different flower houses with cultivated displays of orchids and chrysanthemums that flower all year. The vineyard covers 6 acres, there are wines tastings and guided tours at weekends during the Summer. There is a tea room and a picnic site as well as a gift and wine shop.

Open every day except Christmas Day and New Years Day.

☎ 0622 890561

SEE ALSO *FOOD AND DRINK*

Iden Croft Herbs is one of the largest mixed herb gardens in the country

PARKS & GARDENS

Hever Castle Gardens

Hever, near Edenbridge, Kent

Hever Castle was built as a manor house in 1384 and extended in Tudor times into an elaborate crenellated, moated castle. It was restored at the start of this century by Lord Astor and the present gardens were created by him. The castle was the childhood home of Anne Boleyn. It contains fine panelling in some of its rooms and collections of furniture and paintings. Astor's gardens at Hever are extensive and include a 35 acre lake he created. The gardens' style is Italian Renaissance and their features include a colonnaded piazza, a formal garden with classical sculpture, a topiary and a maze. The grounds also include a mock Tudor village created by Astor. There is a restaurant, a cafe and a shop and Hever hosts open-air theatre during the Summer as well as a range of special events through the year.

Open every day from the middle of March until early November.

☎ 0732 865224

SEE ALSO *HISTORIC BUILDINGS*

Iden Croft Herbs

Staplehurst, Kent

Iden Croft is one of the largest mixed herb gardens in the country. It is surrounded by woodlands and farms. The paths cut through a series of small aromatic and decorative gardens towards the central Victorian Walled Garden. Iden Croft is the home of the national collection of origanum and also has large collections of lavenders, mints, sedum and thyme. There is an information centre and a herb shop with thousands of plants for sale. There is also a tea room. Regular workshops are organised between April and September.

Open every day except Sundays between October and March, it is also closed over the Christmas and New Year period.

☎ 0580 891432

PARKS & GARDENS

Kew Gardens

Kew, Richmond, Surrey
⊖ Kew Gardens

The Royal Botanic Gardens at Kew are one of the finest gardens in the world and a centre of academic excellence. They cover 288 acres and were founded in 1759. The gardens contain more than 25,000 species of plants, shrubs and trees and are crossed by numerous pathways to enable easy access to all parts of the gardens. More delicate species are kept in Kew's three enormous glass conservatories. The Palm House and Temperate House were designed by Decimus Burton in the 19th century. The Palm House recreates the environment of a rain forest whilst the Temperate House contains plants from the Mediterranean area, Africa, New Zealand and the Pacific Islands. The new Princess of Wales Conservatory recreates a variety of different exotic environments in controlled zones. The grounds of Kew contain many follies including ruined temples, a pagoda and the tallest flagstaff in Britain. The work of the Royal Botanic Gardens is explained in exhibitions in the Sir Joseph Banks Building and there are further exhibitions and art displays in the Orangery, the Marianne North Gallery, the Kew Gardens Gallery and Kew Palace. There are shops and restaurants in the gardens.

Closed on Christmas Day and New Years Day.

☎ 081 940 1171

Kew Gardens cover 288 acres and were founded in 1759

Leeds Castle

Near Maidstone, Kent

Leeds Castle looks the very picture of a medieval fortified castle with towers and battlements spanning two islands in the middle of a lake. In fact since Henry VIII's time it has been more a palace than a fortress, in the 1820s it was transformed into a stately home and most of the present collections of furniture, paintings and tapestries were amassed in the 1920s. The formal gardens contain many arrangements of flowers and herbs as well as a croquet lawn, a grotto and a maze. The parkland grounds include pleasant walks and contain a golf course and a vineyard. There is a picnic site in the grounds as well as a tea room, shop and restaurant.

Open every day between April and the end of October, at weekends for the rest of the year and also from 26th December to 1st January.

☎ 0622 765400

SEE ALSO *HISTORIC BUILDINGS* AND *THE REGION AT PLAY*

Leonardslee Gardens

Lower Beeding, near Horsham, West Sussex

Leonardslee covers around 100 acres of valleyside and is set amidst lakes and other water features. It is famous for its camellias and for its rhododendrons and azaleas. It specimen trees include redwoods, oaks, birches and magnolias that are more than 100 years old. The Rock Garden features a waterfall and a wishing well. There is an exhibition of Bonsai trees. The gardens are the home of a herd of sika deer and, surprisingly, a herd of wallabies that have lived on the estate for over 100 years. There is a shop, a restaurant and cafeteria and a picnic site.

Open every day between April and the end of October.

☎ 0403 891212

Marle Place Gardens and Herb Nursery

Brenchley, Kent

10 acres of shrubs and plants set in a garden of lawns and ponds. Marle Place's attraction include an Edwardian rockery planted with herbs, a scented walled garden and a Victorian gazebo. It holds a number of national collections and has a large herb nursery. There is also a woodland area with specimen trees and a streamside walk. There is a shop and a tea room and the gardens contain a picnic site.

Open every day from Easter until the end of October.

☎ 089272 2304

PARKS & GARDENS

Mount Ephraim Gardens

Hernhill, near Faversham, Kent

The gardens cover 7 acres and display a wide range of garden types including a water garden, a Japanese garden, a vineyard, an orchard and woodlands. There are also rose terraces and topiary. In season there are fine displays of daffodils and rhododendrons. The gardens have a craft centre and a tea room and there is a picnic site.

Open every afternoon between mid April and the end of September.

☎ 0227 751496

Nymans Garden

Handcross, near Haywards Heath, West Sussex

The National Trust look after what is regarded by many people as the finest Sussex Weald garden. It covers 30 acres of land surrounding the ruins of an old house. There are many rare trees, shrubs and plants from around the world and stunning displays of rhododendrons, azaleas, magnolias and hydrangeas. The formal gardens include topiary, a laurel walk, a sunken garden and a walled garden. There is a shop and a tea room.

Open every day between April and October except for Fridays and non-Bank Holiday Mondays.

☎ 0444 400321

Parham House

Near Pulborough, West Sussex

The Tudor manor house was built in 1577 and the Great Hall and Long Gallery contain one of the finest collections of Tudor and Stuart paintings in the country. The surrounding grounds at the foot of the South Downs include a deer park with a lake. The formal gardens contain a 4 acre walled garden and an 18th century statuary garden. There is also a maze made of turf and brick. There is a gift shop and a cafe and picnic site.

PARKS & GARDENS

Open between Easter and the start of October except for Tuesdays, Saturdays and non-Bank Holiday Mondays.

☎ 0903 742021

SEE ALSO *HISTORIC BUILDINGS*

Penhurst Place and Gardens

Penhurst, near Tonbridge, Kent

Penhurst is a huge manor house, Sir John de Pulteney started work in the middle of the 14th century, his magnificent Barons' Hall dates from 1341. The rest of the house was mainly completed during the 16th and early 17th centuries. The furniture and paintings in the State Rooms are superb. The present formal gardens were laid out during the 19th century in a 17th century style and include terraces, allees and a parterre. The use made in the gardens of clipped box trees is particularly good. The surrounding parklands feature a nature trail, a lake, an adventure playground and a farm trail. There is a shop and a restaurant.

Open every day from the end of March until early October

☎ 0892 870307

SEE ALSO *HISTORIC BUILDINGS*

PARKS & GARDENS

Petworth House and Park

Petworth, near Midhurst, West Sussex

The present Petworth House was built in the late 17th century in French style for the 6th Duke of Somerset. It contains an impressive collection of paintings including works by Turner, Van Dyck and Lely. The 700 acre deer park was landscaped by Capability Brown in the 1750s and immortalised by Turner's paintings of the Petworth landscape. The park hosts open air concerts in late June. The park and house are maintained by the National Trust and there is a shop and a restaurant on days when the house is open.

The park is open every day except when the open air concerts are performed when it closes at mid day, the house is only open between April and the end of October excluding Fridays and non-Bank Holiday Mondays.

☎ 0798 42207

SEE ALSO *HISTORIC HOUSES*

Mount Ephraim Gardens cover 7 acres and display a wide range of garden types

PARKS & GARDENS

Polesden Lacey

Great Bookham, near Dorking, Surrey

The Regency villa at Polesden Lacey was built in 1824 and the interior was remodelled in Edwardian style in 1906 by the Hon. Mrs. Ronald Greville, it is now run by the National Trust. The extensive grounds include terraces and lawns with box and yew hedges and a range of formal gardens including a walled rose garden, a lavender garden and an iris garden. The grounds also contain an open-air theatre with performances in June and July. There is a picnic site, a shop and a restaurant.

The grounds are open every day, the house is open from Wednesdays to Sundays and Bank Holiday Mondays between April and October and at weekends in March and November.

☎ 0372 458203

SEE ALSO *HISTORIC HOUSES*

Scotney Castle Gardens

Lamberhurst, near Tunbridge Wells, Kent

The National Trust maintain these gardens, they were created in the middle of the 19th century by Edward Hussey who landscaped this hillside area around a ruined 14th century moated castle. It is regarded by many as one of the most romantic gardens in the country and is particularly noted in season for its rhododendrons. The ruins of the castle are opened to visitors during the Summer and there are open air theatre performances by the moat. There is a shop and a picnic area.

The gardens are open every day except Tuesdays and non-Bank Holiday Mondays between April and early November.

☎ 0892 890651

Sheffield Park Gardens

Danehill, near Uckfield, East Sussex

The National Trust maintain this 100 acre garden which was landscaped by Capability Brown in the 18th century. A major feature of the garden is its five lakes, each set at a different height. These lakes feature an array of water lilies. The garden also contains many fine mature specimen trees and in season daffodils and bluebells. It is particularly noted during May and June for its fine displays of rhododendrons and azaleas. There is a shop and a tea room as well as a picnic site.

Open every day between April and early November except for non-Bank Holiday Mondays.

☎ 0825 790655

Sissinghurst Garden

Sissinghurst, near Cranbrook, Kent

The garden at Sissinghurst was created by Vita Sackville-West and her husband Harold Nicolson during this century around the previously derelict remains of an Elizabethan mansion. They started work on the garden in 1930 and today it is one of the most popular gardens in the country and is maintained by the National Trust. It consists of a succession of totally different gardens separated by the walls of the ruined estate. One of the finest of these gardens is the White Garden where every plant is either white or grey in colour. The garden is particularly noted for its rose displays flowering during June and July. Some of the buildings were also restored and the stone tower contains a history of the estate. There is a restaurant and a picnic site and a National Trust shop.

Open every day between April and the middle of October except Mondays.

☎ 0580 712850

Wakehurst Place Garden

Ardingly, near Haywards Heath, West Sussex

Wakehurst covers 600 acres, it is owned by the National Trust and run by Kew Gardens. The gardens are centred on a mansion and include many water features with both lakes and ponds. They are organised as a series of discrete gardens each one featuring important groups of rare and exotic plants, shrubs and trees from around the world. The displays include a section devoted to Himalayan mountain plants, one to American Redwoods and the oldest planted section is the Heath Garden containing plants from Australia and South America, it was first planted in the 1880s. There are also collections of native British and particularly Sussex plantlife including rare wetland habitats and the Loder Valley Nature Reserve. The ground floor of the mansion, which was built in 1590, contains displays and exhibitions and houses a shop. There is a tea room open between Easter and the middle of October.

Open every day except Christmas Day and New Years Day.

☎ 0444 892701

Wilderness Wood

Hadlow Down, near Uckfield, East Sussex

Wilderness Wood is a working wood with traditional chestnut coppices and plantations of pine, beech and fir. There has been a working wood on the 61 acre site for around a 1,000 years and there is an extensive network of paths and rides to follow as well as an organised woodland trail of approximately ¾ of a mile. During the Spring there is also a bluebell trail and around the wood yard there is a tree trail. There is also a woodland play area with an aerial ropeway, a picnic area with barbecues, a tea shop and a gift shop. You can also purchase a range of goods manufactured from the Wood's timber.

Open every day of the year.

☎ 0825 830509

SEE ALSO *WORKING ATTRACTIONS*

PARKS & GARDENS

Winkworth Arboretum

Hascombe, near Godalming, Surrey

Winkworth covers around 100 acres of hillside overlooking two lakes and is planted with an enormous variety of rare trees and shrubs. The planned planting of the specimens creates a glorious combination of colours, particularly in Autumn. Another major feature of Winkworth is its displays of Azaleas and one section of the hillside is planted from top to bottom with different varieties and shades of Azaleas with a stepped trail running through them. There is a shop and a tea room.

The arboretum is open every day, the shop and tea room are open between April and the middle of November except for Mondays.

☎ 0372 453401

Wisley Garden

Wisley, near Woking, Surrey

Wisley is the home of the Royal Horticultural Society and the garden covers 350 acres. It contains the RHS laboratories and experimental areas. Part of the garden is divided in a series of display areas providing examples of almost every style of garden imaginable including gardens that can be created especially for gardeners who are disabled or elderly. In addition to display gardens Wisley also offers guidance and demonstration areas on vegetable and fruit gardening, growing under glass and other areas of interest to practical gardeners. There is a shop and plant centre, a restaurant and cafeteria and a picnic site.

Closed on Sundays and on Christmas Day.

☎ 0483 224234

ANTIQUITIES

Anderida

Pevensey, East Sussex

The substantial ruins of a Roman Saxon Shore fort built in the middle of the 4th century. The massive outer walls and west gate are preserved at heights of up to 28 feet, one of the most impressive Roman remains in this part of the country. The Normans built Pevensey Castle inside the Roman walls and there are major remains of this structure on the site as well. There is a tea room.

Closed on Mondays between the end of September and the end of March,over Christmas and on New Years Day.

☎ 0323 762604

SEE ALSO *Pevensey Castle* IN *HISTORIC BUILDINGS*

Bignor Roman Villa

Bignor, near Pulborough, West Sussex

Bignor is one of the largest Roman villas uncovered in Britain. It was first discovered by chance in 1811 and excavations have revealed more than 60 rooms in the complex. The Roman underfloor heating system is well preserved but the glory of Bignor is its mosaics, regarded by many as amongst the finest anywhere in the world outside Italy. The six major mosaics still retain amazingly strong colours nearly 2,000 years after they were created. There are two formal patterned mosaics including one which, at 82 feet long, is the longest in Britain. The finest of the six is a mosaic of Venus surrounded by cupids dressed as gladiators. The mosaics are all undercover and the site includes a museum, a shop, a cafe and a picnic site.

Closed between November and the end of February and on non-Bank Holiday Mondays in March, April, May and October.

☎ 07987 259

ANTIQUITIES

Fishbourne Roman Palace

Fishbourne, near Chichester, West Sussex

Fishbourne was only uncovered by chance in 1960. Excavation since then has revealed a masterpiece of Roman building and probably the most magnificent Roman dwelling so far uncovered outside Rome. There is no doubting that the building was a palace, it has a formal structure with four distinct wings including one that was reserved for the sole use of visiting Imperial dignities. The remains of the mosaics show them to be amongst the most sophisticated yet discovered and the walls show traces of marble and stucco coverings. The formal gardens have been recreated and planted with the species that would have been growing in Roman times. The palace was built around 50AD probably for Cogidubnus, the pro-Roman King of the Regni, and was occupied until it was destroyed by fire around 280AD. The site includes a museum, a shop, a cafeteria and a picnic site.

Open every day except for the last two weeks in December when it is only open on Sundays.

☎ 0243 785859

Lullingstone Roman Villa

Lullingstone, near Eynsford, Kent

English Heritage look after the remains of this large and impressive villa. It was constructed in the first century AD and was occupied until it was destroyed by fire during the fifth century AD. The remains include a very well preserved bath house and two outstanding mosaic floors. There is also rare evidence of the early conversion of the occupants to Christianity with one of the rooms being the remains of a Christian chapel with a religious wall painting. The entire villa area is enclosed with an audio tape guided walkway and displays of finds at the site includes copies of two busts that are now in the British Museum. There is a shop and a picnic site.

Closed over Christmas and New Year and on Mondays between October and April.

☎ 0322 863467

Pharos

Dover Castle, Dover, Kent

Within the Outer Bailey of Dover Castle, Britain's largest castle, is the Roman Pharos. It is the tallest Roman remain in Britain and was a high tower topped by a beacon to guide cross-Channel shipping into the Roman harbour. When built it reached a height of 80 feet and the first 40 feet are still standing.

Closed on Christmas, Boxing and New Years Days.

☎ 0304 201628

SEE ALSO *DOVER CASTLE* IN *HISTORIC BUILDINGS*

Richborough Castle

Richborough, near Sandwich, Kent

This is regarded as the site of the first successful landing point of the Roman legions that invaded England in 43AD. Named Rutupiae by the Romans it was quickly turned into a fort and supply base. The ditches dug to protect the first fort are just visible on the ground. At the centre of the ruins are the foundations of a huge triumphal white marble arch that Agricola, then Governor of Britain, had erected towards the end of the 1st century to commemorate the capture of the country. A further fortification was built in the 3rd century and its embankments and ditches are clearly visible. The final stage of Roman building happened in the 4th century when a stone Saxon Shore fort was built over the entire site. Parts of the massive outer walls of this fort still stand. English Heritage run a site museum with exhibitions of finds and a gift shop.

Open every day from April until the end of September.

☎ 0304 612013

Roman Painted House

Dover, Kent

The best preserved remains of a Roman town house in the country. Built in the second century AD it contains the earliest known Roman wall paintings in Britain and the remains of the Roman hypocaust or central heating system. The site museum is exceptionally informative and there is a shop.

Closed between November and the end of March and on Mondays in April, September and October.

☎ 0304 203279

Fishbourne Roman Palace was only uncovered by chance in 1960

Alfriston Clergy House

Alfriston, East Sussex

This is a small Wealden hall house, it was built in the 14th century and is half-timbered under a thatch roof. In 1896 it became the first building to be purchased by the National Trust. The building's medieval Hall is particularly fine. There is a permanent exhibition on Wealden building methods and a shop. Outside the house there is a small cottage garden.

Open every day between April and the end of October.

☎ 0323 870001

Arundel Castle

Arundel, West Sussex

The castle was originally built in the 1070s but little remains of the original Norman structure except for part of the south wall and the shell keep. It passed to the Howard family, Dukes of Norfolk and Earl Marshals of England, in 1556 and is still their home. The castle was extensively damaged during the Civil War and was only restored to its present glory by the 15th Duke between 1870 and 1910. The 11th Duke's library containing more than 10,000 volumes

HISTORIC BUILDINGS

is one of the castle's gems. Others include portrait paintings by Gainsborough, Reynolds and Van Dyck. The castle hosts a festival in August each year with an open-air theatre in the grounds. There is a restaurant and a gift shop.

Open every day between April and the end of October except Saturdays.

☎ 0903 883136

Ayleford Friary

Near Maidstone, Kent

The Carmelite friary at Ayleford was founded in the middle of the 13th century on the banks of the River Medway. Following the 16th century dissolution of the monasteries it fell into disrepair before being incorporated into a private house. In 1949 it was re-acquired by the Carmelite order and is once again a friary. The 13th century Pilgrims' Hall has been restored to its former glory and there is also a new large, open-air shrine. There is a pottery in the grounds with a shop. There is also a tea room.

Open every day.

☎ 0622 77272

Arundel Castle was originally built in the 1070s

HISTORIC BUILDINGS

Banqueting House

Horse Guards Avenue, London SW1
⊖ Westminster

The only public building in Whitehall open to the public stands on the site of Henry VIII's Palace of Whitehall. The Banqueting House was added to the Palace in 1622 and was the only part of the Palace to survive a fire in 1698. It was designed by Inigo Jones. Charles I came to the throne and decided the interior needed improving, he commissioned Rubens to paint nine huge paintings to cover the roof, the largest of the paintings has an area of 560 square feet. All nine canvasses were finished and put in place in 1635 and remain so today. Ironically Charles I's rule came to an end when he was beheaded on a platform erected outside on the north wall of the Banqueting House.

Open every day except for Sundays, public holidays and when in use for Government functions.

☎ 071 930 4179

Bateman's

Burwash, East Sussex

Bateman's is delightfully situated in the attractive, wooded Dudwell valley. It was built in 1634 by a Sussex Ironmaster but is best known as Rudyard Kipling's home from 1902 until his death in 1936. Most of the house is preserved as it was on his death, particularly the study where he wrote some of his greatest works. His Rolls Royce is also on display at the house. The charming gardens were mainly Kipling's work. The 18th century mill in the grounds has now been restored as a working attraction. The mill also contains one of the oldest working water turbines in the world, which Kipling had installed to provide the house with electricity. There is a tea room and a shop and there are picnic spots in the grounds.

Open every day between April and the end of October except Thursdays and Fridays.

☎ 0435 882302

SEE ALSO *WORKING ATTRACTIONS*

HISTORIC BUILDINGS

Battle Abbey

Battle, near Hastings, East Sussex

English Heritage maintain the ruins of the great Benedictine Abbey William the Conqueror built on the site of the 1066 Battle of Hastings, or more accurately Battle of Senlac Hill. Building started around 1070 but little remains of the original building. The best preserved remains include the 13th century monks dormitory and the formidable 14th century gatehouse. There is an exhibition and scale model of the battle and diagrams and information boards around the battlefield explain the events that changed England for ever. The church's High Altar is thought to be positioned over the spot where King Harold fell during the battle.

Closed on Christmas, Boxing and New Years Days.

☎ 04246 3792

The best preserved remains of Battle Abbey include the formidable 14th century gatehouse

HISTORIC BUILDINGS

Bayham Abbey

Lamberhurst, Kent

The abbey was founded in 1208 and dissolved in 1525. The substantial ruins are maintained by English Heritage. They include the abbey church, gatehouse and a range of the monks' former quarters and communal rooms. The grounds are in a secluded wooded valley and include a picnic site. There is a tea room and the Abbey hosts a number of open-air events through the year.

Open every day between April and the end of September.

☎ 0892 890381

Bodiam Castle

Bodiam, near Robertsbridge, East Sussex

The National Trust maintain Bodiam. It is regarded by many as one of the finest ruined castles in the country and is the sort of moated, crenellated structure that children dream of when someone mentions the word castle. It was built in 1385 to face French attacks that never came and was "slighted" by Parliamentary Civil War forces in 1643, Lord Curzon undertook some restoration work earlier this century. It is a courtyard castle with a rectangle of high curtain walls linking four cylindrical corner towers, two of the walls have rectangular towers midway along and the other two massive gatehouses. The outer structure is very well preserved and the main gateway still has one of its three original portcullises. The interior is less well preserved but the original Great Hall and other rooms can be distinguished. There is a small museum and shop, a tea room and picnicking in the grounds.

Open every day except for between November and the end of March when it is closed on Sundays, it is also closed over Christmas.

☎ 0580 830436

HISTORIC BUILDINGS

Cabinet War Rooms

King Charles Street, London SW1
⊖ Westminster

The Imperial War Museum administers this suite of 21 underground rooms. They were used by Sir Winston Churchill, his Cabinet and armed services chiefs as the protected nerve centre from which they conducted World War Two and were in continuous use from 1939 until 1945. They have been restored to their appearance during those years and include the Cabinet Room, Transatlantic Telephone Room, Map Room and the Prime Minister's Sitting and Bedroom.

Open every day except for over the Christmas period and New Years Day.

☎ 071 930 6961

HISTORIC BUILDINGS

Carlyle's House

Cheyne Row, London SW3
⊖ Sloane Square

This 18th century Queen Anne style town house on fashionable Cheyne Row was occupied by Thomas and Jane Carlyle from 1834 until their deaths and is now administered by the National Trust. It has been restored to its appearance during their occupancy with personal memorabilia, portraits and books.

Open between April and the end of October from Wednesdays to Sundays and on Bank Holiday Mondays.

☎ 071 352 7087

Chartwell

Near Westerham, Kent

Chartwell is maintained by the National Trust, the house is charming but of no great architectural

HISTORIC BUILDINGS

significance, its position in history is as the country home of Sir Winston Churchill from 1924 until his death in 1965. Displays within the house include Churchill's study. Many rooms have been converted into individual Churchill museums with collections of his uniforms, medals, photographs and the many gifts he received from around the world. The gardens include Churchill's studio, still containing some of his paintings, and the famous brick wall he built personally whilst in the political wilderness. The lakes in the grounds are home to the famous Chartwell black swans. There is a shop and a restaurant.

Open from April until the end of October except for Fridays and non-Bank Holiday Mondays, also open on Wednesdays, Saturdays and Sundays in March and November.

☎ 0732 866368

The Cabinet War Rooms were used by Sir Winston Churchill, his Cabinet and armed services chiefs as the protected nerve centre from which they conducted World War Two

HISTORIC BUILDINGS

Chiswick House

Burlington Lane, London W4
⊖ Turnham Green

The Earl of Burlington built Chiswick House between 1725 and 1729 following a Grand Tour of the continent. It was designed to reflect the architecture of the villas around Venice and with the help of William Kent he created the first Palladian villa in England and caused a major change in English building style. The rooms have their original, if sparse, decorations.

Open every day.

☎ 081 995 0508

Clandon Park

West Clandon, near Guildford, Surrey

The National Trust look after the house in Clandon Park. It was built in the 1730s by the Venetian architect Giacomo Leoni and has a magnificent Marble Hall. The house's furnishings include the Gubbay Collection of porcelain, furniture and needlework. The basement serves as the museum of the Queen's Royal Surrey Regiment and also houses the restored Old Kitchen. the gardens contain a reconstructed Maori meeting house and a grotto. there is a restaurant and a picnic area as well as a shop. There are occasional concerts in the Marble Hall.

The house is open daily except for Thursdays and Fridays between April and the end of October, the park is private.

☎ 0483 222482

Deal Castle

Deal, Kent

Henry VIII built Deal in 1539, it was the largest of the coastal fortifications he created in response to the threat of invasion from the continent and is maintained by English Heritage. It is a symmetrical structure, the tall central circular tower is surrounded by six semicircular low towers which are in turn surrounded by six large semi-circular bastions inside a wide dry moat. An aerial view of the site reveals that the design was modelled on a Tudor rose. The castle was designed and built for artillery and the roofs of the bastions formed gun platforms, in total there are nearly 120 cannon positions in the castle. There are still cannons on the battlements. The keep and gatehouse contain displays of the area's history and the castle's basement houses an exhibition on coastal defences.

Closed on New Years Day.

☎ 0304 372762

Dover Castle

Dover, Kent

Dover Castle dominates the town and coastal approaches from its position on top of the White Cliffs. The Romans recognised the importance of the position and built the Pharos, a lighthouse that is the tallest Roman remain in Britain. The Saxons built a fort on the clifftop position but the Normans started the current bastion. William the Conqueror's motte and bailey castle was replaced by a stone tower in 1180. Henry II, King John and Henry III were responsible for creating the largest castle in Britain and the first concentric castle. The Great Tower's walls are more than feet thick and nearly a 100 feet tall. The Inner Curtain Wall rings the Great Tower and contains 14 towers. The massive Outer Curtain Wall has 20 towers including Constable's Gate, the most elaborate gatehouse in Europe, and encloses an area of 34 acres. As well as the Pharos the grounds include a Saxon church. There are displays throughout the castle including one on the history of the British Army and a model of the Battle of Waterloo. Hellfire Corner is a tour of the underground chambers and tunnels that formed the wartime forward command post during the Second World War. There is a restaurant and a shop.

Closed on Christmas, Boxing and New Years Days.

☎ 0304 201628

SEE ALSO *Pharos* IN *ANTIQUITIES*

Dover Castle dominates the town and coastal approaches from its position on top of the White Cliffs

HISTORIC BUILDINGS

Firle Place

Firle, near Lewes, East Sussex

The original house at Firle was built in Tudor times by Sir John Gage and this building forms the core of the present building which was extended in Georgian style in the middle of the 18th century. The Palladian drawing room is particularly splendid. Firle Place houses an important collection of Old Masters in addition to displays of French furniture and Sevres porcelain. There is an art gallery housing works from local artists, a tea room and shop and a picnic area in the surrounding downland park.

Open over the Easter period and from May to September on Wednesdays, Thursdays, Sundays and Bank Holiday Mondays.

☎ 0273 858355

Goodwood House

Goodwood, near Chichester, West Sussex

Goodwood was rebuilt by James Wyatt in Neo - Classical style in the 18th century for the 3rd Duke of Richmond. The 3rd Duke was also responsible for amassing the collections of Sevres porcelains and Gobelins tapestries and for laying out the house's collection of paintings which includes works by Van Dyck, Lely and Stubbs. There is a tea room and a gift shop and the extensive grounds include the "Glorious Goodwood" Racecourse, Goodwood Golf Club, an equestrian centre and a motor racing circuit as well as nature trails.

The house is open on Sundays and Mondays between mid April and the end of September and also on Tuesdays, Wednesdays and Thursdays in August.

☎ 0243 774107

Great Dixter House and Gardens

Northiam, near Rye, East Sussex

Great Dixter House was built in the 15th century as a large timber-framed manor house. The Great Hall is particularly fine although it was restored at the start of this century by Sir Edwin Lutyens. Lutyens was also responsible for improving the rest of the house and extending it. It houses a collection of antique furniture. Lutyens, working with Gertrude Jekyll, also designed and laid out the delightful gardens. There is a shop selling plants and gifts.

The house and gardens are open in the afternoons between April and the middle of October excluding non-Bank Holiday Mondays; additionally, the gardens are open all day over the Whitsun Bank Holiday Sunday and Monday, all day every Sunday in July and August and all day on the Late Summer Bank Holiday Monday.

☎ 0797 253160

SEE ALSO *PARKS AND GARDENS*

Goodwood House

HISTORIC BUILDINGS

Hampton Court Palace

East Molesey, Surrey

Hampton Court Palace was built by Cardinal Wolsey in 1514 and "given" to Henry VIII in 1529. The original Tudor features were sympathetically extended by Sir Christopher Wren and although much of his work was damaged in a disastrous fire in 1986 it has now been restored. The Great Hall and Chapel Royal are the finest Tudor rooms in the Palace and Wren's beautiful State Apartments are enhanced by the work of Grinling Gibbons and William Kent amongst other. The apartment's contain some of the finest 16th and 17th century paintings in the world. The garden and grounds include formal gardens, water gardens and an Orangery as well as a Wilderness, the Hampton Court Maze and the Great Vine. There is a gift shop, a tea room and picnic spots.

Open every day.

☎ 081 977 8441

SEE ALSO *PARKS AND GARDENS*

Hatchlands

East Clandon, near Guildford, Surrey

The house was built in 1758 for Admiral Boscawen and is now looked after by the National Trust. It was constructed in red brick probably to the Admiral's own design. The interior decoration was the first major commission to be given to Robert Adam and the plasterwork and fireplaces in the drawing room and library are original. The house contains the Cobbe Collection of keyboard instruments and is occasionally the venue for concerts. The surrounding gardens were designed by Gertrude Jekyll and Humphrey Repton. The is a restaurant, a tea room and a shop.

Open on Tuesdays, Wednesdays, Thursdays, Sundays and Bank Holiday Mondays between April and the middle of October.

☎ 0483 222787

HISTORIC BUILDINGS

Hever Castle

Hever, near Edenbridge, Kent

Hever Castle was built as a fortified manor house in 1384 by John de Cobham. During the 15th and 16th centuries it was altered and extended by Sir Geoffrey Boleyn and his grandson Sir Thomas Boleyn and turned into an elaborate crenellated, moated castle. It was the childhood home of Anne Boleyn and is reputedly where she met Henry VIII. It was restored at the start of this century by Lord Astor and the present gardens were created by him. It contains fine panelling and collections of furniture, paintings and other works of art. There is a permanent exhibition on the life of Henry VIII and Anne Boleyn. The gardens are extensive and include a 35 acre lake, a colonnaded piazza, a formal garden with classical sculpture, a topiary and a maze. The grounds also include a mock Tudor village created by Astor. There is a restaurant, a cafe and a shop and Hever hosts open-air theatre during the Summer as well as a range of special events through the year.

Open every day from the middle of March until early November.

☎ 0732 865224

SEE ALSO *PARKS AND GARDENS*

Hever Castle was originally built as a fortified manor house in 1384 by John de Cobham

Ightham Mote

Ivy Hatch, near Sevenoaks, Kent

The National Trust look after this fine small moated manor house. The original house was built in the 1340s in medieval style and now forms one wing of the complete property. The three other wings surrounding the central courtyard were built in the 16th century in Tudor style. Some fine Palladian windows were added to the Drawing Room during the 18th century but the overall external view of the house is that of a well-matured mix of medieval and Tudor, with half-timbered sections, stone sections and brickwork. The interior includes the medieval Great Hall,the Old Chapel with a 14th century crypt, the Tudor Chapel with a ceiling painted in 1520 and the Drawing Room with its windows and fine Jacobean fireplace. There is a tea room and a shop. Ightham Mote is the venue for a series of concerts each July.

Open every day between April and the end of October except Tuesdays and Saturdays.

☎ 0732 810378

Knole

Near Sevenoaks, Kent

Knole has the largest number of rooms contained in any private house in Britain and is now looked after by the National Trust. It was started by Archbishop Bourchier in 1456 and was the property of the Archbishops of Canterbury until Cranmer 'gave' it to Henry VIII in 1538. His daughter Elizabeth I gave Knole to the Sackville family in 1566 and Thomas Sackville started work on extending Knole in 1603. It is still the home of the Sackville family. It is an amazing structure that appears from a distance to be a small hamlet rather than a single house, it contains so many architectural styles. The house contains 365 rooms many of which are richly panelled. The house's paintings include works by Reynolds and Gainsborough, its furniture collection includes many fine 17th century pieces and there are also tapestries and displays of silver. The grounds include a herb garden and a wilderness garden as well as a deer park. There is a tea room and a shop.

The house is open from April to the end of October excluding Tuesdays and non-Bank Holiday Mondays, the park is open every day but the gardens are very restricted and are only open on the first Wednesday of each month between May and September.

☎ 0732 450608

HISTORIC BUILDINGS

Lamb House
Rye, East Sussex

Lamb House is a National Trust property, it is a Georgian townhouse with walled garden and was built in the 18th century. It is most famous for its literary associations. The novelist Henry James lived in the house from 1898 until 1916 and later it became the home of E.F. Benson, creator of the Mapp and Lucia tales. The ground floor rooms house a good collection of James' memorabilia including photographs and letters and contain some of his furnishings.

Open between April and the end of October on Wednesday and Saturday afternoons only.

☎ 0892 890651

Leeds Castle
Near Maidstone, Kent

Leeds Castle looks the very picture of a medieval fortified castle with towers and battlements spanning two islands in the middle of a lake and approached along a causeway through a barbican and a gatehouse. In fact since Henry VIII's time it has been more a palace than a fortress. Building may have started on the site as early as the 9th century but the earliest remains are some stonework in the cellars from the early 12th century. Edward I acquired Leeds in 1278 and the ruined barbican and gatehouse are part of his building work. From Edward II onward it became a favoured residence for English Queens and Henry VIII enlarged the buildings and transformed it by adding palatial new quarters including the Maiden's Tower and the 75 feet long Banqueting Hall. It was further rebuilt and transformed into a stately home in the 1820s and most of the present collections of furniture, paintings and tapestries were amassed in the 1920s. The formal gardens contain many arrangements of flowers and herbs and a maze. The parkland grounds contain a golf course and a vineyard. There is a picnic site in the grounds as well as a tea room, shop and restaurant.

Open every day between April and the end of October, at weekends for the rest of the year and also from 26th December to 1st January.

☎ 0622 765400

SEE ALSO *PARKS AND GARDENS* AND *THE REGION AT PLAY*

Lewes Castle
Lewes, East Sussex

The castle was built in the 1060s shortly after the Norman Conquest but was badly damaged and partially destroyed in 1620. The shell keep was built in the 12th century on one of the two mottes created within the castle grounds and had a commanding position overlooking the town. The ruins can be climbed and there are panels explaining the castle's history. The best preserved part of the castle is its 14th century gatehouse and barbican. There is a shop.

Closed on Christmas and Boxing Days.

☎ 0273 486290

Romantic Leeds Castle

HISTORIC BUILDINGS

Loseley House and Park

Near Guildford, Surrey

The house was built in Elizabethan times and its interior includes panelling thought to have come from Henry VIII's Nonsuch Palace when it was being demolished. Most of the rooms are still furnished in Elizabethan or Jacobean style including the bedroom used by James I. Elizabeth I visited Loseley three times. The most remarkable feature of the house is a fireplace made out of a single piece of carved chalk. The surrounding park is the home of the famous Loseley herd of Jersey cows. There is a restaurant and a shop.

Open from the end of May until the start of October on Wednesdays to Saturdays and on Bank Holiday Mondays.

☎ 0483 304440

SEE ALSO *FOOD AND DRINK*

Maison Dieu

Dover, Kent

Now used as Dover Town Hall, Maison Dieu was founded by Hubert de Burgh, Constable of Dover, in 1203 as a hospice for pilgrims. The interior is magnificent with a beautiful vaulted ceiling and stained glass windows. There are displays of armour and displays on the Lord Wardens of the Cinque Ports. There is also a Book of Remembrance for the men of the Dover Patrol.

Open every day except for Christmas and Boxing Days.

☎ 0304 201200

Marble Hill House

Twickenham, Middlesex

Constructed during the 1720s for George II as a home for his mistress Henrietta Howard, Marble Hill House is one of the finest Palladian villas in the country. It was refurbished in 1901 with a fine collection of 18th century paintings and furniture.

Open every day.

☎ 081 892 5115

Michelham Priory

Upper Dixter, near Hailsham, East Sussex

The Augustine priory of Michelham was built in the early 13th century. In the 14th century the priory's boundary was surrounded by a moat and an impressive gatehouse was built. Following the dissolution of the monasteries most of the priory was destroyed and a Tudor farmer built a magnificent great barn over the ruins. The Prior's house and cellars, the gatehouse, the moat and the great barn all survive. The buildings contain displays of period furniture, tapestries, musical instruments and stained glass. There are also art exhibitions. The grounds include a recreated physic garden containing herbs the monks would have used for medical preparations. The monks' watermill has been restored to working condition. There is a shop, a restaurant and a picnic area.

Open every day between the end of March and the end of October and on Sundays in March and November.

☎ 0323 844224

SEE ALSO *WORKING ATTRACTIONS* AND *THE REGION AT PLAY*

Monk's House

Rodmell, near Lewes, East Sussex

Monk's House is a small Sussex farmhouse and garden owned by the National Trust. In 1919 it became the home of Virginia and Leonard Woolf and it remained in the Woolfs' possession until Leonard died in 1969. The house contains Woolf furniture and memorabilia and the garden's summer house has an exhibition of the Woolfs' lives. The gardens have been restored to they way they were whilst Virginia was alive.

Open between April and the end of October on Wednesday and Saturday afternoons only.

☎ 0892 890651

New Tavern Fort

Gravesend, Kent

The fort overlooks the River Thames and work on it started in the 18th century. At ground level there are gun emplacements which had guns in place guarding the river entrance to London until earlier this century. Below ground there is a complex of tunnels and storage chambers which used to house the guns' ammunition magazines. Some of the chambers have been restored to show what they looked like when in use and others house a special exhibition on life in Gravesend during the Second World War include life-size bomb shelters.

The gun emplacements are open every day, the underground complex is open on Saturdays, Sundays and Bank Holiday Mondays between May and the end of September.

☎ 0474 536995

Osterley Park

Isleworth, Middlesex

The mansion at Osterley Park was originally Elizabethan but was transformed in the 18th century by Robert Adam into one of the finest Neo-Classical villas in the country. It is now administered by the National Trust. Robert Adams transformation of the property was done on behalf of the banker Robert Child and was undertaken between 1760 and 1780. The interior is particularly fine and contains some of the least altered 18th century decoration in the country. The house is surrounded by 140 acres of landscaped parkland. There is a tea room and special events during the year.

HISTORIC BUILDINGS

The house is open between April and the end of October from Wednesday to Sunday and on Bank Holiday Mondays, it is also open at weekends in March, the park is open all year.

☎ 081 560 3918

Pallant House

Chichester, West Sussex

The house was built in the centre of Chichester in Queen Anne style in the 1710s for Henry Peckham, a rich local merchant. For most of this century it was used as local government offices but in the late 1970s and 1980s it was restored to its former glory. The dining room has been returned to the way it would have appeared in the 18th century and the kitchen is an authentic reproduction of how it would have looked in 1900. The house's other rooms hold a remarkable collection of artworks including the Bow Porcelain Collection and the Hussey and Kearley Painting Collections. There is a shop.

Open every day except Sundays and mondays, Good Friday and Christmas and Boxing Days.

☎ 0243 774557

SEE ALSO *MUSEUMS AND ART GALLERIES*

HISTORIC BUILDINGS

Parham House

Near Pulborough, West Sussex

The Tudor manor house at Parham was built in 1577 and with some later modification remains essentially a Tudor and Elizabethan structure. The Great Hall and Long Gallery contain one of the finest collections of Tudor and Stuart paintings in the country including portraits of both Elizabeth I and Henry VIII. The surrounding grounds include a deer park and formal gardens as well as a maze and a lake. There is a gift shop and a cafe.

Open between Easter and the start of October except for Tuesdays, Saturdays and non-Bank Holiday Mondays.

☎ 0903 742021

SEE ALSO *PARKS AND GARDENS*

Penhurst Place and Gardens

Penhurst, near Tonbridge, Kent

Penhurst is a huge manor house built in a variety of styles over hundreds of years. Sir John de Pulteney started the work in the middle of the 14th century, his Barons' Hall dates from 1341 and has a magnificent wooden ceiling and flagstone floor. Buckingham Hall was built next, in the 15th century. The rest of the house was mainly completed during

Pallant House was built in the centre of Chichester in Queen Anne style in the 1710s

HISTORIC BUILDINGS

the 16th and earlier 17th centuries by Sir Henry Sidney and his son. Their work includes the Long Gallery and the Tapestry Room. The Sidneys' still live at Penhurst. The furniture and paintings in the State Rooms are magnificent. The present formal gardens were laid out in the 19th century and the surrounding parklands feature a nature trail, a lake and a farm trail. There is a shop and a restaurant.

Open every day from the end of March until early October

☎ 0892 870307

SEE ALSO *PARKS AND GARDENS*

Petworth House and Park

Petworth, near Midhurst, West Sussex

The present Petworth House was built in the late 17th century in French style for the 6th Duke of Somerset on the foundations of an earlier manor house. The West Front is particularly imposing. The house contains an impressive collection of paintings including works by Turner, Van Dyck and Lely. Turner visited Petworth a number of times in the 1830s and his paintings, including those of Petworth itself, are on display in the Turner Room. The Carved Room is regarded by many as amongst Grinling Gibbons' finest work. The deer park was landscaped by Capability Brown in the 1750s. The park hosts open air concerts in late June. The park and house are maintained by the National Trust and there is a shop and a restaurant on days when the house is open.

The house is open between April and the end of October excluding Fridays and non-Bank Holiday Mondays, the park is open every day although it closes at mid day when the open air concerts are performed.

☎ 0798 42207

SEE ALSO *PARKS AND GARDENS*

HISTORIC BUILDINGS

Pevensey Castle

Pevensey, East Sussex

English Heritage maintain the ruins of Pevensey Castle, they provide as fascinating insight into the vulnerability of the South Coast over the course of 2,000 years of warfare. It was built by the Romans to protect the area from Saxon invasion, rebuilt by the Normans and attacked four times between the 12th and 14th centuries, restored by the Elizabethans in response to the Spanish Armada and restored again this century during the Second World War. There is evidence of each period. The Romans' Saxon Shore fort was built in the 4th century, its Roman name was Anderida and the massive outer walls and west gatehouse still stand. William the Conqueror's son, Robert de Mortain built his Norman castle inside the Roman fort in the late 12th century, parts of the original Norman towers, keep and chapel still exist as do the dungeons. The Elizabethan restoration is represented by displays of cannonballs and catapult balls stockpiled in case the Armada landed in the area. During the Second World War invasion scare the towers were refurbished and the concrete pillboxes and gun emplacements erected at this time are still there. There is a tea room and special events are held at the castle during the Summer.

Pevensey Castle

Closed on Mondays between the end of September and the end of March and over Christmas and New Years Day.

☎ 0323 762604

SEE ALSO *Anderida* IN *ANTIQUITIES*

Polesden Lacey

Great Bookham, near Dorking, Surrey

The Regency villa at Polesden Lacey was built in 1824 and the interior was remodelled in Edwardian style in 1906 by the Hon. Mrs. Ronald Greville. The house contains fine english paintings including works by Reynolds as well as collections of furniture, porcelain and silver. It is run by the National Trust. The extensive grounds include formal gardens and an open-air theatre. there is a picnic site, a shop and a restaurant.

The house is open from Wednesdays to Sundays and Bank Holiday Mondays between April and October and at weekends in March and November, the grounds are open every day.

☎ 0372 458203

SEE ALSO *PARKS AND GARDENS*

Preston Manor

Brighton, East Sussex

The current manor is a Georgian building although there has been a building on the site since the 13th century. The building houses collections of furniture, silver, glassware and ceramics that were amassed by the Stanford family over the 200 years they lived at Preston Manor. There is also a collection of clocks and the Macquoid Bequest of English and Continental furniture and decorative art. The kitchen and various rooms in the servants' quarters including the Butler's Pantry, Servants' Hall and maids' rooms have been restored to the way they would have appeared in Edwardian times. There is a walled garden in the grounds and the manor house has a gift shop.

Closed on non-Bank Holiday Mondays and Good Friday, Christmas and Boxing Days.

☎ 0273 603005

Quebec House

Westerham, Kent

The house was built in the 17th century in red brick with a gabled roof. It is famous as the boyhood home of General Wolfe, the great British soldier who captured Quebec and therefore Canada from the French. Various rooms in the house contain Wolfe family memorabilia and paintings and the Stables contain an exhibition on the Battle of Quebec and the life and death of the General.

Open every afternoon between April and the end of October except for Thursdays and Saturdays.

☎ 0959 562206

HISTORIC BUILDINGS

Rochester Castle

Rochester, Kent

English Heritage maintain the ruins of one of the finest examples of Norman castle architecture in the country. Work on the castle started 1087 and the huge keep was built between 1126 and 1135. Its four stories rise to a height of 113 feet, the south east corner of the keep was rebuilt in the 1220s following an attempt by King John in 1216 to undermine the castle. The rest of the castle apart from some of the original curtain wall was demolished in the early 17th century. There is a shop and a picnic site.

Open every day between April and the end of September, closed on Mondays during the rest of the year and Christmas Eve, Christmas, Boxing and New Years Days.

☎ 0634 402276

Royal Pavilion

Brighton, East Sussex

The then Prince of Wales, later to become Prince Regent and finally George IV, began visiting Brighton in 1783. In 1787 he commissioned Henry Holland to build a summer house. Holland constructed a Neo-Classical seaside villa. In 1815 the Prince decided to extend his Brighton house and commissioned John Nash to undertake the work. By 1822 Nash had completed the Royal Pavilion. The rebuilding was in the style of an Indian Moghul's palace with domes, spires and minarets. The interior is also spectacular with designs borrowing heavily from the Imperial Chinese court. The Music Room and Banqueting Room are particularly splendid. The last monarch to stay at the Royal Pavilion was Queen Victoria, although she did not like the building. Her apartments have been restored and can also be viewed. There is a tea room and a shop.

Closed on Christmas and Boxing Days.

☎ 0273 603005

HISTORIC BUILDINGS

Smallhythe Place

Smallhythe, near Tenterden, Kent

This half-timbered Kentish house was built in the early 16th century. It is best known as the home of the actress Dame Ellen Terry from 1899 until her death in 1928. The National Trust maintains the property as a museum to the actress and it contains a great deal of theatrical and personal memorabilia.

Open every afternoon from April until the end of October except for Thursdays and Fridays.

☎ 05806 2334

HISTORIC BUILDINGS

Squerryes Court

Westerham, Kent

A William and Mary style manor house built in the 1680s. Squerryes Court is still a private house and contains the Wardes family's collections of Old Masters paintings, tapestries and porcelain. General Wolfe of Quebec fame was commissioned into the army at the house at the age of 14 and there is a collection of Wolfe memorabilia. The grounds include formal gardens, a lake and woodlands. There is a tea room.

Open on Wednesday, Saturday, Sunday and Bank Holiday Monday afternoons between April and the end of September and on Sunday afternoons in March.

☎ 0959 562345

Squerryes Court contains the Wardes family's collections of Old Masters paintings, tapestries and porcelain

HISTORIC BUILDINGS

Standen

Near East Grinstead, West Sussex

The National Trust look after this house which was designed and built by Philip Webb in 1894. Webb was a close friend of William Morris and Standen is the only house he designed that has remained more or less unaltered including some of his original light fittings. Morris provided some of the house's textiles and wallpapers and they were amongst his first wallpaper designs. The surrounding gardens are on a hillside overlooking the Medway valley and contain woodland walks. There is a shop, a tea room and picnic sites.

Open every day between April and the end of October except for Tuesdays and non-Bank Holiday Mondays.

☎ 0342 323029

Tower of London

Tower Hill, London EC3
⊖ Tower Hill

Probably one of the most famous and most photographed castles in the world, the Tower of London was started by William the Conqueror in 1067 to control the citizens of London following the Norman Conquest. The central White Tower was built between 1078 and 1097. The original stone Tower was further strengthened in the 13th century when Henry III surrounded it with a curtain wall linking 13 towers and his son Edward I surrounded this with an outer curtain wall linked by a further six towers, creating an impregnable fortress which he further enhanced by enclosing the whole in a moat. Over the centuries it has been a royal palace, prison, zoo and place of execution. Today it is was of the most visited tourist attractions in the country and the home of the Crown Jewels, the Beefeaters and the famous Ravens. There is a shop.

Open every day.

☎ 071 709 0765

Walmer Castle

Walmer, Kent

Walmer was built by Henry VIII during the 1530s, it has a similar layout to Deal Castle although the central tower is only surrounded by four bastions. The castle's structure was modified in the 18th century when it was converted from a fortress into the palatial official residence of the Lord Wardens of the Cinque Ports. The apartments are panelled and furnished and there are displays relating to the lives of famous past Lord Wardens including the Duke of Wellington who died at Walmer in 1852. The castle is surrounded by terraced gardens. There is a shop.

Open every day between April and the end of September and Wednesdays to Sundays for the rest of the year except when the present Lord Warden, the Queen Mother, is in residence.

☎ 0304 364288

Tower of London

RELIGIOUS BUILDINGS

Canterbury Cathedral

Canterbury, Kent

Canterbury's christian associations date back to St. Augustine in 597AD. The present cathedral was founded by Archbishop Lanfranc in 1070, the crypt is the largest Norman crypt in the world. Thomas a Becket was murdered in the cathedral in 1170 and in 1174 it was badly damaged by fire. William of Sens started rebuilding work immediately after the fire although the last element, the North West Tower, was not completed until 1840. Canterbury is the mother church of the Church of England and contains the tombs of more than 50 Archbishops. Its most famous memorial is the armoured effigy of the Black Prince. The cathedral has a gift shop.

Open every day except for when services are underway.

☎ 0227 762862

Chichester Cathedral

Chichester, West Sussex

The present cathedral was started in 1088 but displays building styles from Norman to the 19th century as well as fine 20th century religious artworks including tapestry by John Piper and paintings by Graham Sutherland. There are shops and a cafe and the cathedral hosts musical events.

Open every day except when services are underway.

☎ 0243 782595

Guildford Cathedral

Guildford, Surrey

Guildford is a 20th century cathedral built of red brick in a simplified Gothic style. It was designed by Sir Edward Maufe and was constructed between 1936 and 1961. It is particularly noted for its glasswork and needlework. It has a brass rubbing centre, a shop and a cafe.

Open every day

☎ 0483 65287

RELIGIOUS BUILDINGS

Rochester Cathedral

Rochester, Kent

The See of Rochester was founded in 604AD, only Canterbury was founded earlier. The present building was started in 1082 by Bishop Gundolf although the original Norman structure was modified in the Early English Perpendicular style during the 12th and 13th centuries. The Norman West Door and the 13th century Choir Stalls are particularly impressive. The visitor centre at the cathedral has a shop and sells refreshments.

Open all year.

☎ 0634 843366

St. Paul's Cathedral

Ludgate Hill, London EC4

⊖ St. Paul's

There has been a church on this site since the 6th century and a huge Norman cathedral occupied it from 1087 until 2nd September 1666 when it was badly damaged during the Great Fire of London. The ruins were demolished and Sir Christopher Wren was commissioned to build a replacement. The result is a masterpiece, the only domed cathedral in Britain. Stunning though the architecture and interior decoration is the cathedral's crypt is probably its most fascinating area.

RELIGIOUS BUILDINGS

Running the whole length of the building it is the largest crypt in Europe and is the last resting place of many great English and British heros. Amongst its tombs two of the finest are those of Admiral Lord Nelson and the Duke of Wellington. There is a shop.

Open every day unless services or formal duties are underway.

☎ 071 248 2705

Westminster Abbey

Parliament Square, London SW1

⊖ Westminster

The present Westminster Abbey, really the Collegiate Church of St. Peter Westminster, was built by Edward the Confessor between 1050 and 1065. William the Conqueror consolidated his victory at Hastings by crowning himself King of England in the Abbey on Christmas Day 1066. In doing so he created a precedent and every subsequent monarch but two have had their coronation in the Abbey. The building is a Gothic masterpiece and the Nave is the tallest and one of the greatest in the country. There is a museum and a brass rubbing centre.

Open every day unless services or formal duties are underway.

☎ 071 222 5152

The See of Rochester was founded in 604AD, only Canterbury was founded earlier

MUSEUMS & ART GALLERIES

Arundel Toy and Military Museum

Arundel, West Sussex

Set in a Georgian cottage in the heart of Arundel is a delightful museum full of dolls, teddy bears and toy soldiers. There are also displays of dolls' houses, military models and toy farms and boats. There is a gift shop.

Open every weekend, Bank Holidays and every every day between the middle of June and the middle of September.

☎ 0903 882908

Bank of England Museum

Bartholomew Lane, London EC2
⊖ Bank

The Bank of England has existed since 1694 and the museum, which is housed within the bank, tells its story. There are displays, interactive videos and period reconstructions as well as documents from well-known historic customers of the bank. The are also displays on the current role of the bank and the ways international banking and finance work. There is a shop.

Open every day except for Saturdays, Christmas Day, Boxing Day, New Years Day and Sundays in Winter.

☎ 071 601 5545

Bentley Wildfowl and Motor Museum

Bentley, near Lewes, East Sussex

Bentley House contains the Philip Rickman Collection of Wildfowl Paintings and is the home of a museum of roadworthy vintage cars. There is a miniature steam railway in the grounds. Bentley has the largest private collection of wildfowl in Britain. There is a gift shop, a tea room and a picnic site.

Open every day between the

MUSEUMS & ART GALLERIES

middle of March early September, the grounds only are also open at weekends except for during January.

☎ 0825 840573

SEE ALSO *WILDLIFE*

British Engineerium

Hove, East Sussex

The British Engineerium exhibition is housed in the old Goldstone Pumping Station, built by the Victorians on the edge of the South Downs to pump water for Brighton and Hove. The brickwork building has a chimney 100 feet tall and contains thousands of engineering exhibits ranging from engineers' models and hand tools to full-size working steam engines. The largest exhibit is the pumping station's own original 1876 beam engine, it has been fully restored and is in steam every Sunday and Bank Holiday. There is a shop.

Open every day except between the 18th and 28th of December.

☎ 0273 559583

British Engineerium

MUSEUMS & ART GALLERIES

British Museum

Great Russell Street, London WC1
⊖ Tottenham Court Road

The British Museum was founded around the collections of Sir Hans Sloane in 1753. It is one of the world's truly great museums and has collections ranging from Assyrian, Egyptian and Greek antiquities through Roman mosaics and artefacts to Medieval treasures. The collection of original handwritten scripts in the Manuscript Saloon is priceless and the British Museum Reading Room with its famous domed ceiling has been a place of research and motivation for many of the world's great thinkers. There is a museum shop and a cafeteria.

Open every day.

☎ 071 636 1555

Brooklands Museum

Weybridge, Surrey

The Brooklands Circuit was created in 1907 by Hugh Locke King and rightly describes itself as the birthplace of British motorsport and aviation. Brooklands' heydays were in the 1920s and 1930s with notable drivers such as Malcolm Campbell and although racing was stopped by World War Two the aviation links continued until 1987. The museum is continuing to develop and expand. The most recent development is the opening of Malcolm Campbell's original work sheds, built in 1926 they have been fully restored and now house Brooklands' main car collection. The aviation exhibits include a Hawker Harrier, the Sultan of Oman's personalised VC10 and the famous Wellington raised from Loch Ness. Brooklands hosts more than 40 motoring and aviation event days a year ranging from gatherings of car collector club members to 24 hour kart races and light aircraft fly-ins. There is a restaurant and a shop.

Open at weekends only from October to March and every day for the rest of the year except for non-Bank Holiday Mondays.

☎ 0932 857381

C. M. Booth Collection of Historic Vehicles

Rolvenden, Kent

The collection's centrepiece is a unique display of Morgan cars from 1913 to 1935 but there are also other early makes of car as well as motor cycles and bicycles. The collection also includes model cars and a range of automobilia. There is a gift shop.

Open except for Sundays and Christmas Day and Boxing Day.

☎ 0580 241234

Design Museum

Butler's Wharf, London SE1
⊖ Tower Hill

A relatively new museum opened in 1989 to show the development and influence of design in mass production. It covers everything from perfume to motor cars and looks not just at the design of the product but also at the accompanying advertising and promotion from a design perspective. There is a special section on graphics as well as displays and reviews of new products and a changing programme of special exhibitions on specific areas of design. There is a shop and a riverside cafe.

Open every day except for non-Bank Holiday Mondays.

☎ 071 403 6933

The British Museum is one of the world's truly great museums

MUSEUMS & ART GALLERIES

Dickens House Museum

Doughty Street, London WC1
⊖ Chancery Lane

Charles Dickens lived here between 1837 and 1839, during which period he completed Pickwick Papers, wrote Oliver Twist and Nicholas Nickleby and started work on Barnaby Rudge. The building contains the finest collection of Dickens memorabilia in the world and a number of first editions. There is a shop.

Open every day except for Sundays.

☎ 071 405 2127

Dulwich Picture Gallery

College Road, London SE21

One of the finest private picture galleries in the world. The gallery was designed by Sir John Soane and the 13 rooms house a magnificent collection of Old Masters including 17th century works by Rembrandt, Rubens, Murillo and Van Dyck and 18th century work by Gainsborough, Canaletto, Reynolds and Hogarth. There is a museum shop.

Open every day except for Mondays and public holidays.

☎ 081 693 5254

MUSEUMS & ART GALLERIES

Ethnic Doll and Toy Museum

Whitstable, Kent

Whitstable Castle gatehouse houses this exhibition of authentic ethnic dolls from around the world. There are other displays including dolls' houses and teddy bears. There is a working model railway, a shop and a cafe.

Open every day from the end of January to 22nd December.

☎ 0227 771456

Florence Nightingale Museum

Lambeth Palace Road, London SE1
⊖ Waterloo

Housed in one of the buildings of St. Thomas's Hospital this museum tells the story of Florence Nightingale's pioneering work to improve the standards and conditions of nursing. There is also a display on the development of modern nursing techniques. The museum's centrepiece is a reconstruction of Nightingale's famous ward at Scutari during the Crimea War.

Open every day except for Mondays.

☎ 071 620 0374

The Florence Nightingale Museum tells the story of Florence Nightingale's pioneering work

MUSEUMS & ART GALLERIES

Fort Amherst

Chatham, Kent

A Napoleonic fort covering 14 acres, it was built in 1756 as one of the major guardians of Chatham Dockyards. The bastions and redoubts with their gun batteries and the network of 2,500 feet of tunnels connecting and supplying them are being restored. There are a range of displays including a working gun battery. There is a shop and a cafeteria as well as a picnic site.

Open every day except for 22nd December to 3rd January.

☎ 0634 847747

Freud Museum

Maresfield Gardens, London NW3
⊖ Finchley Road

The psychoanalyst Sigmund Freud is normally associated with his home in Vienna. However, in 1938 Freud fled to London following the Nazi takeover of Austria. He moved into a house in Elsworthy Road and his family used the furnishings from their apartment in Vienna to create an exact duplicate of the working environment of their Austrian home in this house in Maresfield Road in leafy Hampstead. Freud worked in the house and his final two works were written here. He died a year later on 23rd September 1938 and his daughter Anna arranged for the house to be used as a museum following her death in 1982. The house contains Freud's famous couch, his desk, his library and working papers and his fine collection of antiquities. There is a shop and temporary exhibitions on different aspects of Freud's life and work.

Open every day except for Mondays and Tuesdays.

☎ 071 435 2002

MUSEUMS & ART GALLERIES

Hastings Embroidery

Hastings, East Sussex

Created by artists at the Royal School of Needlework in 1966 to commemorate the 900th anniversary of the Battle of Hastings. The Hastings Embroidery is 245 feet long and illustrates every major event to have happened in British history between 1066 and 1966. There is also a model of the Battle of Hastings and a small shop.

Closed on Saturdays and Sundays and all Bank Holidays.

Historic Dockyard

Chatham, Kent

Chatham Royal Dockyard was founded by Henry VIII in 1547 and began building ships for the Royal Navy in 1586 with the launching of the Sunne. It constructed more than 400 vessels including Nelson's Victory and the last ship to be built in Chatham was the submarine Ocelot, launched in 1962. Since 1984 the dockyard has been looked after by the Chatham Historic Dockyard Trust and the 80 acre site is now the most completely preserved Georgian dockyard in the world. The buildings and exhibits around the dockyard tell the story of life in the dockyard from the Commissioner and his officers to the everyday dockyard workers. There are seven major attractions including a 1/4 mile long working ropery. There is a shop and a cafeteria, a tea shop in Summer and picnic sites. There are special events throughout the year.

A scene from the How We Lived Then Museum

MUSEUMS & ART GALLERIES

Open on Wednesdays, Saturdays and Sundays between the end of October and the end of March and every day for the rest of the year except for Tuesdays and non-Bank Holiday Mondays.

☎ 0634 812551

Horniman Museum

Forest Hill, London SE21

Fredrick Horniman founded this museum in the 1880s as an exhibition of the natural environments, cultures, arts, crafts and music of the world. The collections are quite diverse and include an impressive collection of masks and puppets, a display of musical instruments from around the world and natural history displays including aquaria. There is a museum shop and a cafe. The museum is surrounded by 16 acres of parkland and hosts special events throughout the year and concerts of world and ethnic music.

Open every day.

☎ 081 699 1872

How We Lived Then Museum of Shops and Social History

Eastbourne, East Sussex

An 1850 Late Regency style town house is the setting for a display of the typical wares of more than 20 different types of shops as they were between 1850 and 1950. The shops include a grocers, a chemists, a tailors, an ironmongers, a post office, a jewellers and a toy shop. There is also a real gift shop.

Open every day.

☎ 0323 737143

MUSEUMS & ART GALLERIES

Imperial War Museum

Lambeth Road, London SE1

⊖ Lambeth North

A museum devoted totally to telling the story of warfare in the 20th century and, because of its subject matter, a continuously expanding and changing museum. The current range of exhibits cover warfare from World War One to the Gulf War. There are fine displays of military and warfare paintings, mostly from official war artists. There are specially themed high technology displays including Blitz which tells the story of life in wartime London in World War Two. There are also a large number of historic military documents one of the most recent of which is the Argentinian Surrender Document from the Falklands War and a great deal of military memorabilia. There is a museum shop and a cafe.

Open every day.

☎ 071 416 5000

Kenwood House

Kenwood, London NW3

⊖ Golders Green

Kenwood House was built in the 17th century and remodelled by Robert Adam in Neo - Classical style in the 1760s. During the 1920s it was bought by Lord Iveagh and filled with his art collection. On his death in 1927 he bequeathed the house and the collection to the nation. Features of the collection include works by Turner, Gainsborough, Reynolds, Rembrandt, Van Dyck and Vermeer. There is a shop and a cafe. The house is set in 74 acres of grounds including a lake and during the Summer there are open air concerts alongside the lake.

Open every day.

☎ 081 348 1286

MUSEUMS & ART GALLERIES

Kew Bridge Steam Museum

Brentford, Middlesex
⊖ Gunnersbury

Housed within the Victorian pumping station serving the whole of west London is one of the finest displays of working stationary steam engines in the world. Grand Junction 90 is a Cornish beam engine and, with its 90 inch beam, is the largest working beam engine in the world, it is in steam every weekend. Alongside it is Grand Junction 100, it is in the process of restoration and one day its 100 inch beam will be in steam again. There are seven other steam engines in displays around the site and a working diesel engine as well as the restored small gauge steam railway that used to serve the pumping works, it runs once a month and on special event days. There is also a museum devoted to the history of water supply in London. There is a book shop and a tea room at weekends and there are special events throughout the year.

Open every day but in steam only at weekends and on Bank Holidays.

☎ 081 568 4757

London Toy and Model Museum

Craven Hill, London W2
⊖ Paddington

An impressive display of more than 7,000 commercially made toys and models ranging from an ancient Roman gladiator doll to a modern toy robot. Displays include teddy bears, dolls and dolls' houses as well as model trains, Dinky cars, Meccano kits and model soldiers. The gardens house a miniature railway, a vintage roundabout and a model double decker bus. There is a shop and a cafe and there are special events throughout the Summer.

Open every day.

☎ 071 262 9450

London Transport Museum

Covent Garden, London WC2
⊖ Covent Garden

Housed in the former Flower Market of old Covent Garden this museum tells the history of transport in London. There is an extensive collection of vehicles including vintage buses, trolley buses and steam locomotives. There are video displays including the driver's view from a speeding tube train and many "hands on" displays as well as collections of London Transport's most famous posters. There is a shop.

The museum is normally open every day except for Christmas Day and Boxing Day but will be closed until the end of December 1993 for work to be undertaken.

☎ 071 379 6344

Museum of London

London Wall, London EC2
⊖ Barbican

This is the largest museum in the world devoted to a single city and tells the story of London from the time approximately 400,000 years ago when the first hunter-gatherers arrived in the Thames Valley to the present day. The city itself was founded by the Romans around 50AD and displays in the museum recreate

all the major moments in the history of the metropolis over nearly 2,000 years. The great state and civic roles of London are displayed with, for example, the magnificent Lord Mayor's coaches but so to is everyday life and work in London across the centuries. There is a museum shop, a restaurant and coffee house and special events throughout the year.

Open every day except for non-Bank Holiday Mondays.

☎ 071 600 3699

Museum of the Moving Image

South Bank, London SE1
⊖ Waterloo

A relatively new museum, opened in 1988, and devoted to the history of the moving image from Chinese shadow theatre to electronic news gathering and fibre optic technology. The museum's emphasis is on the use of image in cinema and television and its is a very modern, practical museum with a large number of "hands on" exhibits, demonstrations and activities. The museum is part of the South Bank Arts Complex and shares their range of shops and cafes.

Open every day

☎ 071 928 3535

A typical exhibit at the London Toy Museum

MUSEUMS & ART GALLERIES

National Army Museum

Royal Hospital Road, London SW3
⊖ Sloane Square

The history of the British army from 1485, when Henry VII raised the first Yeomen of the Guard, to 1982, the end of the Falklands War. There are displays of uniforms, weapons and medals as well as a wide range of military memorabilia including items as diverse as the complete skeleton of Napoleon's favourite charger and Lord Raglan purpose-built telescope for use with one arm. There is a shop and a cafe.

Open every day except for Good Friday and Christmas, Boxing and New Years Day.

☎ 071 928 3535

National Gallery

Trafalgar Square, London WC2
⊖ Charing Cross

The National Gallery is the home of one of the world's great art collections. It was founded in 1824 and moved into its present site in 1838. The collection has grown rapidly since then and the opening of the latest major extension to the site, The Sainsbury Wing, in 1991 has allowed the entire collection to be rehung. The gallery houses over 2,000 major works including examples of the work of almost every major artist from the 15th century to the start of the 20th century. It is impossible to summarise the range of masterpieces in the National Gallery but, as a taster, two of the English paintings in the collection are Constable's The Hay Wain and Turner's The Fighting Temeraire. There is a museum shop and restaurant and there are special exhibitions.

Open every day except for Good Friday and Christmas, Boxing and New Years Day.

☎ 071 839 3321

National Maritime Museum

Romney Road, Greenwich, London SE10

Britain's premier maritime museum tells the history of the role of the sea and seafaring in the life of the nation. There are large displays of ships, ship models, weapons, uniforms, figureheads, globes, telescopes and marine paintings. There are special sections on two of Britain's best known sailors, Nelson and Cook. The grounds of the museum also house Inigo Jones' Queen's House and the Old Royal Observatory with its museum of astronomy and time. There are special displays and exhibitions at the museum. There is a shop and a cafe.

Open every day except for Good Friday, Christmas Day, Boxing Day and New Years Day.

☎ 081 858 4422

Alfred Waterhouse's imposing Victorian building is the home of the Natural History Museum

National Portrait Gallery

St. Martin's Place, London WC2
⊖ Leicester Square

Portraits, busts and photographs of famous and important people from the Middle Ages to the present day. There are always about 1,000 images on display but the total collection is much larger. There are varying temporary displays and exhibitions. There is a museum shop.

Open every day except for Good Friday, Christmas and Boxing Day and New Years Day.

☎ 071 306 0055

Natural History Museum

Cromwell Road, London SW7
⊖ South Kensington

Alfred Waterhouse's imposing Victorian building is the home of the Natural History Museum. The collection was started as part of Sir Hans Sloane's bequest that created the British Museum but the natural history section was separated in the 1880s to form its own museum. The museum's displays cover all aspects of natural history including geology, evolution and ecology. There are exhibitions devoted to dinosaurs, whales, and other special types of creatures. There is a shop and a restaurant.

Open every day except for Good Friday, over the Christmas period and New Years Day.

☎ 071 938 9123

MUSEUMS & ART GALLERIES

Pallant House

Chichester, West Sussex

The Queen Anne style house was restored in the late 1970s and 1980s. The dining room has been returned to the way it would have appeared in the 18th century and the kitchen is an authentic reproduction of how it would have looked in 1900. The house holds a remarkable collection of artworks including the Bow Porcelain Collection and the Hussey and Kearley Painting Collections. Walter Hussey was the Dean of Chichester Cathedral responsible for commissioning most of its modern artworks and his personal collection at Pallant House includes John Piper's original sketches for his tapestries and a portrait of Hussey by Graham Sutherland. There is a shop.

Open every day except Sundays and Mondays, Good Friday and Christmas and Boxing Days.

☎ 0243 774557

SEE ALSO *HISTORIC HOUSES*

Powell-Cotton Museum

Birchington, Kent

Quex House, a Regency mansion with Victorian additions, houses the collections of Major Horace Powell-Cotton. He spent most of his life travelling the world and the nine galleries contain his trophies from Africa, Asia and America. The animals are displayed in realistic natural settings and include White Rhinos and Elephants. There are displays of native artefacts and weapons. There is also a collection of Chinese Imperial porcelain and a cannon captured from the French in Canada. There is a gift shop and during Summer months a tea room.

Open Sundays all year and also on Wednesdays, Thursdays and Bank Holiday Mondays between April and October.

☎ 0843 42168

MUSEUMS & ART GALLERIES

Redoubt Fortress

Eastbourne, East Sussex

Built during the Napoleonic invasion scares the fortress has been fully restored and houses the museums of the Royal Sussex Regiment and the Queen's Own Irish Hussars and well as displays on the history of martello towers, the cinque ports and the coastguards. There is also an underground aquarium. The fortress hosts open air concerts during the Summer. There is a shop and a cafeteria.

Open every day between Easter and early November.

☎ 0323 410300

Royal Air Force Museum

Hendon, London NW9
⊖ Colindale

An impressive display of more than 60 aircraft associated with the development of military aviation in this country. There are also exhibitions of aviation memorabilia and special presentations on the work of Bomber Command in World War Two and on the Battle of Britain with reconstructions of life on a fighter base and in a fighter control room. There is a shop and a restaurant.

Open every day except for Good Friday, over the Christmas period and New Years Day.

☎ 081 205 2266

MUSEUMS & ART GALLERIES

Royal Engineers Museum

Gillingham, Kent

Housed in the Brompton Barracks this museum of Britain's soldier-engineers tells the story of their role in war and peace throughout the centuries. There are special displays on two illustrious Royal Engineers, Gordon of Khartoum and Lord Kitchener. The courtyard is occupied by a Harrier jump jet. There is a shop and a cafe as well as a picnic site.

Open every day except for Fridays, New Years Day, Christmas Day and Boxing Day.

☎ 0634 406397

Science Museum

Exhibition Road, London SW7
⊖ South Kensington

The Science Museum was founded by the Victorians in 1875 and now houses more than 60 different galleries looking at every aspect of science and technology. Some of the galleries are huge and hold steam locomotives and space rockets and many of the exhibits are "hands on" so that people can gain a greater understanding of how and why things work. The Science Museum is also the home of the Wellcome Museum of the History of Medicine, one of the largest exhibitions of its type in the world.

Pallant House

Open every day except for Good Friday, over the Christmas period and New Years Day.

☎ 071 938 8000

Shakespeare Globe Museum

Bear Gardens, London SE1
⊖ London Bridge

The Globe Theatre on Bankside was the site of the performance of the works of Shakespeare and other contemporary Elizabethan playwrights, it was built around 1598 and closed in 1642. Sam Wannamaker has been instrumental in the revitalisation of interest in Elizabethan Bankside and the creation of the International Shakespeare Globe Centre which is in the process of constructing a full size replica of the theatre using Elizabethan building techniques. When complete Shakespeare "in the round" will once more return to Southwark. In the meantime the company operates the Shakespeare Globe Museum in Bear Gardens. The museum tells the story of Elizabethan theatre and Bankside and also has displays devoted to the work of archeologists in uncovering the remains of the Globe and the nearby Rose Theatre. It also houses a reconstruction of a 17th century indoor or "private" theatre and a shop.

Open every day.

☎ 071 928 6342

Shipwreck Heritage Centre

Hastings, East Sussex

A modern "sound and light show" museum set on a medieval ship in a simulated dock and telling the story of a shipwreck that happened 500 years ago. There are also displays on "Roman and Later Treasures from Shipwrecks". There is a gift shop.
Open every day from Easter until the end of September.

☎ 0424 437452

Sussex Toy and Model Museum

Brighton, East Sussex

Housed in the arches underneath Brighton railway station is a delightful museum with collections of toy and model soldiers, dolls, cars, trains and planes. There is a tea room and a shop.

Open every day except for non-Bank Holiday Mondays.

Tangmere Military Aviation Museum

Tangmere, near Chichester, West Sussex

A former Battle of Britain fighter station now housing a museum covering the history of aerial warfare. Aircraft on display include a Hawker Hunter and an American T33. One exhibition area presents the story of the base during its 50 years of active service as an RAF Station, another the story of the Battle of Britain. There is a special display on the Dambusters raid with a reconstruction of the Mohne Dam site. There are also working models and a flight simulator as well as displays of uniforms, medals and military memorabilia. There is a gift shop, a cafe and a picnic site.

Open every day between February and the end of November.

☎ 0243 775223

Tate Gallery

Millbank, London SW1
⊖ Pimlico

The Tate Gallery opened in 1897 and was given to the nation by Sir Henry Tate. It houses the national collection of British painting from the 16th century to the present day and a world-ranking collection of international 20th century works. The gallery is completely rehung at least once a year so the actual works on display vary a great deal but they are all outstanding. The Tate is also the home of the Clore Gallery which opened in 1987. On his death Turner left to the nation all of the paintings that were still in his studio, on the condition that they should be hung together, the Clore Gallery is the home of this collection. There is a shop, a restaurant and many special exhibitions.

Open every day except for Good Friday, over the Christmas period and New Years Day.

Theatre Museum

Tavistock Street, London WC2
⊖ Covent Garden

Opened in 1987, the Theatre Museum is really devoted to all forms of performance and includes ballet, dance, opera, circus, mime, rock and pop and music hall. There are special displays of memorabilia, costumes, props and billboards. There is a shop, a box office for theatre bookings and a cafe.

Open every day except for Mondays.

☎ 071 836 7891

Toy and Model Museum

Lamberhurst, Kent

An oast house has been converted into a museum featuring dolls and teddy bears. There is a special section on Rupert the Bear as well as displays of model cars, a model fairground and a model railway. The complex also includes a village street with period shops and a craft centre. There is a tea room and a picnic site.

Open every day except for Christmas Day.

☎ 0892 890711

MUSEUMS & ART GALLERIES

Tyrwhitt-Drake Museum of Carriages

Maidstone, Kent

Housed in the medieval stables of Maidstone's Archbishop's Palace is a unique collection of more than 50 carriages. They range from simple trader's carts and sedan chairs to royal carriages and some date from as early as the 17th century. There is a small shop and a picnic site.

Open every day except for Sundays, New Years Day, Good Friday and Christmas and Boxing Days.

☎ 0622 754497

Victoria and Albert Museum

Cromwell Road, London SW7
⊖ South Kensington

Created by the Victorians as a museum of ornamental art the Victoria and Albert is one of the world's great museums with superb collections of European and Oriental decorative and fine arts from the 15th century to the present day. The collections include paintings, jewellery, needlework, fashion, sculpture and ceramics. There are also displays of musical instruments and applied arts. There is a shop and a restaurant and there are regular special events and special exhibitions.

Open every day except for Good Friday,over the Christmas period and New Years Day.

☎ 071 938 8500

Weald and Downland Open Air Museum

Singleton, near Chichester, West Sussex

A rare collection of historic buildings that have been preserved, brought to the museum and re-erected in their original state. The buildings range from medieval cottages to a working 17th century watermill and are centred around a preserved farmhouse. There are woodland trails and walks around the museum, a shop, a cafe and a number of picnic sites. There are special events during the Summer.

Open every day between March and the end of October and on Sundays and Wednesdays during the rest of the year.

☎ 024363 348

The Victoria and Albert Museum

WORKING ATTRACTIONS

Bartley Mill

Bells Yew Green, near Frant, East Sussex

The watermill dates from the 13th century and was owned by the monks of nearby Bayham Abbey it was once part of a thriving hop farm but ceased milling in the early 1900s and has only recently been restored to working order. It mills organically grown wholemeal flour from its own farm. Local bakers turn this into a variety of foods including six different types of breads which are for sale in the shop. There is also a small museum, a tea room and a picnic area.

Open every day except for Christmas Day and New Years Day.

☎ 0892 890372

Badsell Park Farm

Matfield, near Tonbridge, Kent

A working arable farm specialising in wheat, sweetcorn and fruit. The changing activities on the farm through the growing and harvesting and picking seasons can be observed. There is a farm trail and a woodland and meadow nature trail. There is also a pets and farm animals corner, a gift shop, picnic sites and a cafe. During the season there are "pick your own" facilities.

Open every day between the end of March and the end of November.

☎ 0892 832549

Bateman's

Burwash, East Sussex

Bateman's was built in 1634 by a Sussex Ironmaster but is best known as Rudyard Kipling's home from 1902 until his death in 1936. Various rooms including his study are open and his Rolls Royce is also on display at the house. The charming gardens were mainly Kipling's work. The 18th century mill in the grounds has now been restored as a working attraction. It is used to grind corn into wholemeal flour and the flour is for sale at the house. The mill grinds corn once a week. The mill also contains one of the oldest working water turbines in the world, which Kipling had installed to provide the house with electricity. There is a tea room and a shop and there are picnic spots in the grounds.

Open every day between April and the end of October except Thursdays and Fridays, the mill grinds corn every Sunday at 2 p.m. during the open months.

☎ 0435 882302

SEE ALSO *HISTORIC BUILDINGS*

Children's World and Farm

Beckley, near Rye, East Sussex

A 600 acre working dairy and hop farm. There is a farm trail leading you around the farm's animals, milking and feeding sessions and a working blacksmith to watch. There is a children's theatre and an adventure playground as well as a trekking centre and a grass carting track. The shop sells farm produce, craft goods and antiques. There is a tea room and a picnic site.

Open every day between April and September and at weekends in March.

☎ 0797 260250

Dungeness Nuclear Power Stations

Dungeness, Kent

The information centre has exhibitions and displays on the principles of generating electricity using nuclear power and the story of the stations. It is also the starting point for guided tours of the complex including the control room, the core and the generator hall. There is a gift shop and a cafe.

Open every day except for over the Christmas and New Year period.

☎ 0679 21815

Bartley Mill

WORKING ATTRACTIONS

Eurotunnel Exhibition Centre

Cheriton, near Folkestone, Kent

The centre is sited close to the UK terminus of the Channel Tunnel. The tunnel is one of the largest construction projects ever undertaken. A physical link between Britain and the continent has been dreamed about for centuries, construction started in 1987 and the first breakthrough was made on 30th October 1990, commercial services should be running through the tunnel some time during 1994. The exhibition tells the story of the construction, explains about the tunnel's strategic importance in the European transport grid and enables visitors to simulate what an actual journey through the tunnel will be like. There is also a large N-gauge model railway of the terminal and an observation tower. There is a shop and a picnic site and the centre's cafe is, naturally, french-style.

Open every day except for non-Bank Holiday Mondays between the middle of October and the end of March.

☎ 0303 270111

TheEurotunnel Exhibition Centre

Michelham Priory

Upper Dixter, near Hailsham, East Sussex

The Augustine priory was built in the early 13th century although the gatehouse and moat are 14th century. A Tudor great barn was built over part of the site after the dissolution of the monasteries. The Prior's house and cellars, the gatehouse, the moat and the great barn all survive and contain displays of period furniture, tapestries, musical instruments, stained glass and art exhibitions. The grounds include a recreated physic garden containing herbs the monks would have used for medical preparations. The monks' watermill was fed by water from the River Cuckmere, it has been restored to working condition and grinds corn which is sold in the shop. There is also a restaurant and a picnic site in the grounds.

Open every day between the end of March and the end of October and on Sundays in March and November.

☎ 0323 844224

SEE ALSO *HISTORIC BUILDINGS* AND *THE REGION AT PLAY*

Thames Barrier

Woolwich, London SE18

In order to prevent tidal surges up the River Thames flooding central London it was decided that some form of barrier had to be created, one tall enough and strong enough to stop a huge body of water but at the same time one which would allow shipping to pass through unheeded. The result was the Thames Barrier, in normal conditions all that can be seen above water are nine huge piers, each one resembling a humpbacked whale. Underwater there are eight gates on pivots, in times of flood alert they can be swung through 90 degrees to link to each pier and form an impenetrable barrier 60 feet high across the width of the Thames. Building work started in 1974 and the barrier was completed in 1984. The barrier has been raised 14 times in response to flood warnings since it was completed 9 years ago. On the south bank of the barrier is the Thames Barrier Visitor Centre with a 10 minute video and an 18 minute multi media show on various aspects of the construction and work of the barrier and a series of displays. There is a viewing gallery overlooking the barrier and a pier with boat trips around the barrier and up river to Greenwich and central London. There is a shop and a cafe.

Open every day.

☎ 081 854 1373

Wilderness Wood

Hadlow Down, near Uckfield, East Sussex

Wilderness Wood is a family-owned working wood with traditional chestnut coppices and plantations of pine, beech and fir. There has been a working wood on the 61 acre site for around a 1,000 years. You can see trees in various stages of growth and being harvested. The barn in the wood yard provides displays and demonstrations on the various uses of wood from Wilderness Woodland you can purchase garden furniture, picnic tables, garden decorations and other timber products in the yard. There is an extensive network of paths and rides in the wood as well as an organised woodland trail of approximately ¾ of a mile and a shorter tree trail. During the Spring there is also a bluebell trail. There is also a woodland play area with an aerial ropeway, a picnic area with barbecues, a tea shop and a gift shop.

Open every day of the year.

☎ 0825 830509

SEE ALSO *PARKS AND GARDENS*

STEAM RAILWAYS

Bluebell Railway

Sheffield Park, near Uckfield, East Sussex

A 7 1/2 mile preserved steam railway line running from Sheffield Park to Horsted Keynes and Newcombe Bridge. The line reopened in 1960 after it was rescued by enthusiasts. The steam locomotives on the line were built between the 1860s and the 1950s and are the largest collection of working locomotives in the south east of England. Sheffield Park Station has been restored to its appearance in the 1880s and includes a museum, shops and a restaurant. Horsted Keynes Station has been refurbished in a 1930s style and has a bar and bookstall. The locomotives' rolling stock includes Pullman restaurant cars at weekends.

Open on Sundays all year, Saturdays between March and December and every day from late May until the end of September.

☎ 082572 2370

Kent and East Sussex Steam Railway

Kent and East Sussex Steam Railway

Tenterden, Kent

The single track line runs for 7 miles from Tenterden to Northiam with stops at Rolvenden and Wittershaw Road. The line was built in the late 1890s, closed by British Rail in the 1960s and reopened by enthusiasts in 1974. There are 16 steam locomotives used on the line and housed in the engine sheds at Rolvenden, the oldest of them, Sutton, was built in 1876. The rolling stock includes the

STEAM RAILWAYS

Victorian Train and the London and North Western Railway Director's Saloon. Tenterden Station has been refurbished in Edwardian style and features a display area, museum, gift shop and buffet. The trains carry restaurant cars on Saturday evenings and Sunday lunchtimes during the Summer and there is a tea room at Northiam and picnic sites at both ends of the line. There are special event days throughout the year including Friends of Thomas the Tank Engine Weekends in June and September.

The line is working every Sunday except during January, on Saturdays from April until early November and every day from June until the end of September.

☎ 0580 765155

Romney, Hythe and Dymchurch Railway

New Romney, Kent

A unique railway line running for 14 miles across Romney Marshes from Hythe to Dungeness and stopping at four intermediate stations including New Romney. The line and locomotives are all built at one third normal scale and it is the world's smallest public railway. There are eleven steam locomotives and two diesel units running on the line and in Summer there are up to 12 trains a day. New Romney is the headquarters of the railway and home of the workshops and engine sheds, the station has a gift shop and buffet as well as a picnic site, a childrens' playground and a toy and model museum. There is also a cafe at Dungeness and certain trains carry a licensed observation car. There are a number of special events during the Summer.

Trains run every day from April until the end of September and at weekends from late February until the end of October.

☎ 0679 62353

FOOD & DRINK

Barkham Manor Vineyard

Piltdown, near Uckfield, East Sussex

The vineyard covers 35 acres of rolling downland around Barkham Manor House and was the site of the discovery of the Piltdown Man hoax. It was planted in 1985 and the English wines it produces frequently win international awards. The vineyard's winery is one of the most modern in Europe. There are guided tours and a vineyard trail. There are also organised wine tastings and wine appreciation courses. The 1750 thatched Great Barn has been restored and incorporates a shop that sells the wines and a wide range of gifts and souvenirs.

Open every day between April and 24th December except for non-Bank Holiday Mondays.

☎ 0825 722103

Biddenden Vineyard

Biddenden, near Ashford, Kent

An 18 acre vineyard established in 1969 on south - facing slopes. Biddenden produces a range of award winning white and rose wines as well as a number of strong Kent ciders. There are guided tours of the vineyard and winery with wine tastings during June, July and August. During the rest of the year visitors can roam the vineyard on their own before visiting the shop.

Closed from Christmas Eve until 2nd January and on Sundays in January and February.

☎ 0580 291726

Carr Taylor Vineyard

Westfield, near Hastings, East Sussex

Award winning sparkling and still white wines are produced by this 37 acre vineyard. Set on south-facing downland slopes the estate also contains bluebell woods. The winery also produces a number of special limited-edition wines including an Indian wine created using a traditional recipe combining exotic ingredients with the basic wine. There are organised tours, wine tastings and, for children, a fun worksheet on the vineyard. There is a shop.

Open every day between April and Christmas Eve and all weekends between January and April.

☎ 0424 752501

The Carr Taylor Vineyard

FOOD & DRINK

Denbies Wine Estate

Dorking, Surrey

The largest vineyards in Britain cover an area of 250 acres and produce a range of wines. The winery also houses a visitor centre which is the starting point for a presentation on wine making and an audio guided tour of the winery and estate. There is a restaurant and a picnic area as well as a wine shop.

Open every day from April until the end of December except for Christmas Day.

☎ 0306 876616

Headcorn Flower Centre and Vineyard

Headcorn, Kent

The vineyard covers 6 acres and visitors can stroll around it, there are wine tastings and guided tours at weekends during the Summer. The flower houses contain spectacular displays all year. There is a tea room and a picnic site as well as a gift and wine shop.

Open every day except Christmas Day and New Years Day.

☎ 0622 890561

SEE ALSO *PARKS AND GARDENS*

Lamberhurst Vineyard

Lamberhurst, near Tunbridge Wells, Kent

A large vineyard covering 50 acres and producing a range of English wines. There is a vineyard trail and there are organised tours of the winery and cellar. There is a restaurant and a picnic site. The wine shop also sells a range of local produce.

Open every day except for Christmas Day, Boxing Day and New Years Day.

☎ 0892 890286

FOOD & DRINK

Loseley House and Park

Near Guildford, Surrey

The house was built in Elizabethan times. Most of the rooms are still furnished in Elizabethan or Jacobean styles. The most remarkable feature of the house is a fireplace made out of a single piece of carved chalk. The surrounding park is a working farm, the home of the famous Loseley herd of Jersey cows. There are also rare breeds of pigs, sheep and poultry. There are farm tours and milking demonstrations and the farm shop sells the Loseley Jersey range of dairy products. There is also a restaurant.

Open from the end of May until the start of October on Wednesdays to Saturdays and on Bank Holiday Mondays.

☎ 0483 304440

SEE ALSO *HISTORIC HOUSES*

Lurgashall Winery

Lurgashall, near Petworth, West Sussex

The winery makes country wines as well as English Mead and a range of liqueurs. The entire production process can be viewed and there is also a museum and display on wine making and a herb garden. The winery shop sells a range of local produce and gifts as well as the drinks.

Open every weekend of the year.

☎ 0428 707292

Penhurst Vineyards

Penhurst, near Tunbridge Wells, Kent

The vineyards covers 12 acres, they were first planted in 1972 and produces a range of award winning wines. Visitors are welcome to roam around the vineyards, there are guided tours of the modern winery

FOOD & DRINK

which features a carved wooden 4,000 litre cask and wine tastings. Penhurst also produces apple wine and apple juice from its own orchards. There is a wine shop. The vineyards are also the home of some interesting wildlife including a herd of wallabies.

Closed at weekends in January and February and over the Christmas and New Year period.

☎ 0892 870255

SEE ALSO *WILDLIFE*

St. George's Vineyard

Waldron, near Heathfield, East Sussex

The vineyard was first planted in 1979 on an ancient estate listed in the Domesday book. It covers 20 acres and produces a variety of white and rose wines including a sparkling one. There are vineyard tours and wine tastings and many special events during the year. St. George's run an "adopt-a-vine" scheme and has a restaurant and a snack bar. The shop is housed in an 11th century tithe barn and sells a wide range of local produce as well as the wines.

Open every day in July and August and between December 4th and 23rd, every day except non-Bank Holiday Mondays between April and the end of October and at weekends for the rest of the year.

☎ 043 53 2156

St. George's Vineyard

WILDLIFE

Bentley Wildfowl and Motor Museum

Bentley, near Lewes, East Sussex

Bentley House is surrounded by 100 acres of gardens featuring lakes and ponds. The estate houses a wildfowl collection that was started by Gerald Askew, it is the largest private wildfowl collection in Britain and is the home of more than 1,000 birds representing more than 115 species of wildfowl from around the world including representatives of every type of swan in the world. The species also include Australian shelducks, Hawaiian geese and Thai wood ducks. The house contains the Philip Rickman Collection of Wildfowl Paintings, a collection of more than 150 wildfowl water colours, as well as a museum of roadworthy vintage cars. There is a children's adventure playground and a miniature steam train, a gift shop, a tea room and a picnic site.

The grounds are open every day between the middle of March and early September and every weekend except for during January, the house is only open from the middle of March until early September.

☎ 0825 840573

SEE ALSO *MUSEUMS AND ART GALLERIES*

Birdland

Near Farnham, Surrey

Birdland's 20 acres house displays of more than 1,000 birds including many exotic species such as flamingos, toucans and emus, the lake encloses a penguin island. A second feature of Birdland is Underwaterworld, an aquarium holding an interesting range of exotic fish. There are gift shops, a cafe and snack bar and a picnic area.

Open every day except for Christmas Day.

☎ 0420 22140

WILDLIFE

Blean Bird Park

Blean, near Canterbury, Kent

The park is the home of one of the country's largest breeding collections of macaws as well as flocks of cockatoos, parrots and pheasants. There is a children's play area and a woodland walk. There is a cafe, a tea room and a picnic site as well as a shop.

Open every day except Christmas and Boxing Days.

☎ 0227 471666

Brambles Wildlife and Rare Breeds

Near Herne, Kent

Animals ranging from rabbits to wallabies and wild cats live in nearly 30 acres of park and woodland. There are also aviaries and a collection of English rare breeds. There is children's playground and a shop as well as a tea room and a picnic area.

Open every day from April to the end of October.

☎ 0227 712379

Blean Bird Park

WILDLIFE

Brighton Sealife Centre

Brighton, East Sussex

There are more than 30 separate aquatic displays at the centre including a shark display with an underwater tunnel as a viewing platform. There is a gift shop and a coffee shop.

Open every day except for Christmas Day.

☎ 0273 604234

Chessington World of Adventures Zoo

Chessington, Surrey

Chessington Zoo was transformed in 1987 when the old zoo site became a theme park and as part of the park a new zoo area with large landscaped enclosures was created. The zoo plays an important role in breeding endangered species including Lowland Gorillas and Snow Leopards. The zoo has a Reptile House and a Birdland as well as a Children's Zoo. Chessington World of Adventures is themed into nine separate areas with a wide range of white knuckle rides and attractions. There are refreshment sites and shops.

Brighton Sealife Centre

WILDLIFE

The zoo is open every day except for between 24th December and 1st January, the theme park is open every day between the end of March and the end of October.

☎ 0372 727227

SEE ALSO *THE REGION AT PLAY*

Chilham Castle Gardens Raptor Centre and Petland

Chilham, near Canterbury, Kent

The 250 acre estate surrounding Chilham Castle includes an 18th century deer park, and 17th century formal gardens containing the King Holm Oak, an evergreen oak on the upper lawn that was planted in 1616 to mark the completion of the new mansion and is still growing. The Raptor Centre for birds of prey was created in 1977. The birds can be seen on their weathering ground from mid day and performing flying displays in the afternoons every day the gardens are open except Mondays and Fridays. Petland in the orchard is the home of a wide range of small domestic animals and birds. There is a gift shop and a tea room and picnic site. There are special events at weekends throughout the Summer.

WILDLIFE

Open every day between April and mid October.

☎ 0227 730319

SEE ALSO *PARKS AND GARDENS*

Drusillas Park

Near Alfriston, East Sussex

Drusillas Park houses an interesting and varied collection of wild animals and birds in modern, large enclosures. The collections include a number of species of monkey including some rare breeds. There are also meerkats, llamas, penguins and parrots and special areas devoted to beavers, otters and owls. Drusillas Park was founded over 60 years ago and the complex includes craft workshops, a variety of family entertainments and shops. There is a pub, a restaurant, a snack bar and a picnic site.

Open every day except for Christmas and Boxing Days.

☎ 0323 870234

SEE ALSO *THE REGION AT PLAY*

Gatwick Zoo

Charlwood, near Crawley, Surrey

The zoo's 10 acres of landscaped grounds contain a varied display of animals and birds many of which have been successfully bred at the zoo. Monkey Island houses the zoo's breeding troop of squirrel monkeys. The aviary is a walk-through free-flight enclosure about 80 feet long with many exotic species including macaws. There is also a free-flight butterfly house which is temperature controlled to resemble jungle conditions and houses many species of tropical butterflies. There is a gift shop, a cafe and a picnic area.

Open every day except for Christmas and Boxing Days.

☎ 0293 862312

WILDLIFE

Howletts Zoo Park
Bekesbourne, near Canterbury, Kent

Howletts was opened by John Aspinall in 1975 to display his collection of rare breeds from around the world. From the start he intended it to be an important breeding centre and today it has one of the largest collections of tigers in the world and one of the largest of breeding gorillas. It was also the first zoo in this country to breed African elephants successfully. The park is centred on a fine 18th century mansion with a magnificent entrance portico.

Open every day except Christmas Day.

☎ 0227 721286

London Zoo
Regent's Park, London NW1
⊖ Camden Town

London Zoo, or more accurately the Zoological Society of London, was founded in 1826 as the world's first public zoo. Decimus Burton erected the first buildings and it opened in 1827. Although currently the centre of much controversy over its financing and future role in the changing world of animal conservation and care it is still a major attraction with thousands of animals in enclosures which still include the 1913 Mappin Terraces and the 1965 Snowdon Aviary. There is a shop and there are cafes.

Open every day except Christmas Day.

☎ 071 722 3333

Penhurst Vineyards
Penhurst, near Tunbridge Wells, Kent

The vineyards covers 12 acres, they were first planted in 1972 and produces a range of award winning wines. They are home for an interesting range of wildlife including black swans, rare breeds of sheep and, unusually, a herd of wallabies. Visitors are welcome to roam around the vineyards and there are also guided tours of the grounds and the modern winery. Penhurst also produces apple wine and apple juice from its own orchards. There is a wine shop and there are wine tastings.

Closed at weekends in January and February and over the Christmas and New Year period.

☎ 0892 870255

SEE ALSO *FOOD AND DRINK*

Port Lympne Zoo Park
Lympne, near Hythe, Kent

The Port Lympne estate was bought by John Aspinall as an overflow site for his Howletts Zoo Park. The 300 acres of landscaped park contain a series of open reserves housing herds of rare breeds ranging from deer and antelope to rhinoceroses and elephants. The estate's mansion was built by Sir Herbert Baker in 1911 in Dutch Colonial style and has displays relating to the zoo park including a wildlife art gallery. There is a visitor centre, a shop selling gifts and craft goods, a restaurant and picnic areas.

Open every day except for Christmas Day.

☎ 0303 264646

Rare Farm Animals of Hollanden
Hildenborough, near Sevenoaks, Kent

The farm is a sanctuary for rare breeds of a range of British farm animals including horses, cattle, sheep, goats and pigs. It also looks after rare breeds of chickens and a variety of waterfowl. There is a woodland and water trail, an adventure playground and a farm shop. There is also a tea room and a picnic site.

Open every day from the end of March until early October.

☎ 0732 832276

South of England Rare Breeds Centre
Woodchurch, near Ashford, Kent

A working farm is the home of this major rare breeds centre that looks

The Arundel Wildfowl and Wetlands Centre provides a home for more than 1,000 swans, geese, ducks and other wildfowl

WILDLIFE

after more than 60 different species of rare farm animals. There is a farm animal corner specially for children with tame cattle, pigs and sheep and a nature trail. There is also a farm trail and a woodland trail. There is a gift and farm shop, a restaurant and a picnic area.

Open every day except for Christmas Day.

☎ 0233 861494

Sussex Farm Museum

Horam, near Heathfield, East Sussex

The museum is devoted to farming and country life. There is a woodland walk, a nature trail and a countryside interpretation centre as well as demonstrations of country crafts and old farming methods. There is a restaurant and a picnic area.

Open every day between Easter and the end of October.

☎ 04353 2597

Wildfowl and Wetlands Centre

Arundel, West Sussex

The Wildfowl and Wetlands Trust owns 60 acres of lakes and water meadows alongside the River Arun below Arundel Castle. These provide a home for more than 1,000 swans, geese, ducks and other wildfowl. There is a viewing gallery overlooking the central lake and seven hides dotted around the grounds as well as gravel pathways through the centre. There is a visitor centre with a cinema and gift shop, a restaurant and a picnic site. There are special events and talks throughout the year.

Open every day except Christmas Day.

☎ 0903 883355

THE REGION AT PLAY

A Day At The Wells

Tunbridge Wells, Kent

A "state of the art" audio visual reconstruction of a day's visit to Tunbridge Wells on a sunny Summer's day in 1740. Built inside the restored Corn Exchange, the day starts at a coaching inn in Southwark, London, just before the coach to Tunbridge Wells departs and includes scenes in the Coffee House, strolling along the Pantiles, taking the waters and preparing for the evening's ball. There is a gift shop.

Open every day except Christmas Day.

☎ 0892 546545

A Day At The Wells

THE REGION AT PLAY

Buckleys Yesterday's World

Battle, East Sussex

Housed in Wealden Hall House in the centre of Battle, Buckleys recreates a wide range of everyday scenes from 1850 to 1950. Individual room represent a chemist's shop, a grocers, a sweet shop, a Victorian kitchen, a photographer's studio and a nursery. There is also a reconstructed 1930s railway station. The garden terrace invites you to enjoy a cream tea whilst looking over a typical English Country Garden and there is a special Childrens' Play Village and working model fairground. There is a shop and a picnic site.

Open every day except Christmas Day and New Years Day.

☎ 0424 775378

Canterbury Tales

Canterbury, Kent

A "state of the art" audio visual presentation of the 14th century pilgrims' journey from London's Tabard Inn to Becket's Tomb in Canterbury Cathedral with vivid presentations of Chaucer's Tales. The exhibition is built within medieval St. Margaret's Church and includes a shop and coffee shop.

Open every day except Christmas Day.

☎ 0227 454888

Chessington World of Adventures

Chessington, Surrey

The theme park at Chessington was created in 1987 by transforming the site of Chessington Zoo into a series of nine themed entertainment areas. The nine are Transylvania, The Mystic East, Calamity Canyon, English Market Square, The 5th Dimension, Smugglers Cove, Toytown, Circus World and Animal Areas. There are a wide range of white knuckle rides including the Vampire and the Runaway Train and many other attractions and entertainments. The Animal Areas are the redesigned home of the original Chessington Zoo and the animal collections play an active role in the breeding of endangered species. There are shops and restaurants throughout the complex.

Chessington World of Adventures is open every day between the end of March and the end of October, the Animal Areas Zoo is open every day except for between 24th December and 1st January.

☎ 0372 727227

SEE ALSO *WILDLIFE*

Cutty Sark

King William Walk, Greenwich, London SE10

The Cutty Sark was one of the great clipper ships that used to race back from Australia to England loaded with 5,000 bales of wool in her holds. She was launched in 1869 and was used to bring tea back from China before being switched to the lucrative wool run. She is now kept in dry dock on the Greenwich riverside and was recently remasted as part of a major overhaul. The lower deck houses a collection of ship's figureheads and you can also view the crew and officers quarters. Close alongside also in dry dock is Gypsy Moth IV, the ship in which Sir Francis Chichester sailed single handed around the world in 1966.

Cutty Sark is open every day, Gypsy Moth IV is only open between April and October.

☎ 081 858 3445

Dickens Centre

Rochester, Kent

The Dickens Centre recreates scenes from Charles Dickens' books using models and special effects. There is also an audio visual presentation of the author's life and work and a collection of Dickens first editions. The centre's grounds house the Swiss chalet he used as a study when he lived at nearby Gad's Hill Place.

Open every day except for Christmas and Boxing Days.

☎ 0634 844176

Chessington World of Adventures was created in 1987 by transforming the site of Chessington Zoo

THE REGION AT PLAY

Drusillas Park

Near Alfriston, East Sussex

Drusillas Park was founded over 60 years ago as a tea room and today offers a wide range of attractions. There is a zoo with an interesting and varied collection of wild animals and birds in landscaped, modern, large enclosures, a farmyard with friendly animals and "Mildred" a life size model cow that can be milked. The craft workshops in Drusillas Village including a pottery and The Whackey Paint Shop where visitors can screen print their own designs on to T shirts. There is also a miniature railway and a huge adventure playground. Drusillas has eight shops selling a wide range of gifts and souvenirs, a pub, a restaurant, a snack bar and a picnic site.

Open every day except for Christmas and Boxing Days.

☎ 0323 870234

SEE ALSO *WILDLIFE*

Fort Fun and Rocky's Adventure Land

Eastbourne, East Sussex

A 2 acre fun park designed especially for the under 12s, Fort Fun has a wide range of exciting rides and attractions. Rocky's Adventure Land is a new extension especially created for the under 5s and is an enchanting yet totally safe area for the young adventurer. There is a cafe and a picnic area.

Rocky's Adventure World is open every day except Christmas and Boxing Days, Fort Fun is open over Easter, at weekends from April to the end of October and every day from July until the middle of September.

☎ 0323 642833

THE REGION AT PLAY

Fort Luton Museum

Chatham, Kent

A Victorian fort that has been restored and now houses a museum and a model railway. The 4 1/2 acres of grounds contain an adventure playground, a pets corner and a collection of "silly sculptures" as well as gardens. There is a craft shop, a cafe and a picnic site.

Open every day from March until Christmas Eve.

☎ 0634 813969

Guinness World of Records

The Trocadero, Coventry Street, London W1

⊖ Piccadilly Circus

A presentation of some of the most impressive and most visual records from the Guinness Book of Records using life sized models, videos, multi screen audiovisuals and high tech effects. There is also a shop.

Open every day except Christmas Day.

☎ 071 439 7331

THE REGION AT PLAY

HMS Belfast

Tooley Street, London SE1

⊖ London Bridge

This Royal Navy cruiser was built in 1936, it is the largest preserved warship in Europe and is permanently moored on the south bank of the Thames across the river from the Tower of London. The ship is administered by the Imperial War Museum and visitors can inspect the engine rooms, the control room, the mess decks, the gun turrets and the bridge. There is a shop and a cafe.

Open every day except Christmas Day.

☎ 071 407 6434

The London Dungeon recreates the Victorian East End of Jack the Ripper

THE REGION AT PLAY

Leeds Castle

Near Maidstone, Kent

Leeds Castle looks like a medieval fortified castle with towers and a moat but since Henry VIII's time it has been more a palace than a fortress, in the 1820s it was transformed into a stately home and most of the present collections of furniture, paintings and tapestries were amassed in the 1920s. The formal gardens contain many arrangements of flowers and herbs as well as a croquet lawn, a grotto and a maze. There are also aviaries full of exotic birds, a duckery and black swans on the lake. The parkland grounds include pleasant walks and contain a 9-hole golf course and a vineyard. The gatehouse is home to a very unusual museum devoted to collecting dog collars, some of which are up to 400 years old. There is a picnic site in the grounds as well as a tea room, shop and restaurant.

Open every day between April and the end of October, at weekends for the rest of the year and also from 26th December to 1st January.

☎ 0622 765400

SEE ALSO *PARKS AND GARDENS* AND *HISTORIC BUILDINGS*

London Dungeon

Tooley Street, London SE1

⊖ London Bridge

Britain's only horror themed adventure depicting torture, death and superstition. The high tech effects make everything shockingly realistic and it is definitely not for the weak hearted. The life size reconstructions of executions are very impressive. The latest addition is a recreation of the Victorian East End of Jack the Ripper. There is a shop and a cafe.

Open every day.

☎ 071 403 0606

THE REGION AT PLAY

THE REGION AT PLAY

London Planetarium

Marylebone Road, London NW1
⊖ Baker Street

The London Planetarium still offers observation of the planets and stars via projection onto the inside of the dome. But nowadays the computerised high tech Starburst shows, which last for 30 minutes, are preceded by Space Trail, a new lift off zone with interactive video monitors featuring live satellite communication before you "reach" the observation platform for Starburst.

Open every day except for Christmas Day.

☎ 071 486 1121

Madame Tussaud's

Marylebone Road, London NW1
⊖ Baker Street

Madame Tussaud's is the world's largest waxworks and has been established in London since 1833 and based in the present buildings since 1884. Alongside the traditional galleries of the famous and the infamous there are now many specially created tableaux and an exciting new history of London. The Spirit of London opened for the first time in Spring 1993 and cost over £10 million. It is a "time taxi" ride through London experiencing the sights, sounds and smells of the great moments of London history using wax figures, audio-animatronic figures and high tech computers. The journey takes you through 400 years from Elizabethan London to the present day. There is a shop and a cafe.

Open every day except Christmas Day.

☎ 071 935 6861

Madame Tussaud's

Michelham Priory

Upper Dixter, near Hailsham, East Sussex

The Augustine priory was built in the early 13th century although the gatehouse and moat are 14th century. A Tudor great barn was built over part of the site after the dissolution of the monasteries. The Prior's house and cellars, the gatehouse, the moat and the great barn all survive and contain displays of period furniture, tapestries, musical instruments, stained glass and art exhibitions. The grounds include a recreated physic garden containing herbs the monks would have used for medical preparations. The great barn is used to house a museum of the work of blacksmiths and wheelwrights and also has a display on rope making. The monks' watermill was fed by water from the River Cuckmere, it has been restored to working condition and grinds corn which is sold in the shop alongside various local craft works. There is also a restaurant and a picnic site in the grounds. During the Summer there are often special events at Michelham Priory.

Open every day between the end of March and the end of October and on Sundays in March and November.

☎ 0323 844224

SEE ALSO *HISTORIC BUILDINGS* AND *WORKING ATTRACTIONS*

Palace Pier

Brighton, East Sussex

The Palace Pier was built in 1899 and is the most popular seaside pier in the country. There is plenty to see and do along its length including rides, dodgems and amusement arcades or you can just stretch out in a deckchair, take the sun and watch the world go by. There are fast food outlets and bars and, in restored full Victorian splendour, the Palm Court Fish Restaurant.

Open every day.

☎ 0273 609361

Rock Circus

Piccadilly Circus, London W1
⊖ Piccadilly Circus

A rock and pop themed entertainment creating using wax models and audio-animatronic figures and the technological know-how of the experts from Madame Tussaud's. There are more than 50 figures recreating the story and music of rock and pop from the 1950s to the 1990s and ranging from Bill Haley, Little Richard and Elvis to Madonna and Bono. As well as the fixed displays the revolving stage presents four sets of different groups of stars introduced by Tim Rice's commentary. There is a shop and a cafe.

Open every day.

☎ 071 734 7203

THE REGION AT PLAY

Smart's Amusement Park

Littlehampton, West Sussex

A long-established South Coast entertainments complex with rides and attractions for all the family including rollercoasters, dodgems and funfair rides. There is also a gift shop, a cafe and a picnic site.

Open every day from April until the end of September.

☎ 0903 721200

Smugglers Adventure

St. Clements Caves, Hastings, East Sussex

The caves cover 1½ acres, were used by real smugglers in the 18th century and have had wide and varied uses over the last 200 years including a military hospital, a ballroom, an air raid shelter, a wax works and a jazz club. In 1989 they re-opened as a state-of-the-art exhibition of the history of smuggling with more than 50 life size figures, automated models and sound and light effects. The ballroom has also been restored to the way it would have appeared in the 1820s and there is a display on the history of the caves. There is a shop.

Open every day except for Christmas Day.

☎ 0424 422964

Spitting Image Rubberworks

James Street, London WC2

⊖ Covent Garden

An exhibition of the famous rubber figures and robotic caricatures created especially for the Spitting Image TV shows. There is also a tour of the workshops where the models are made and a shop.

Open every day.

☎ 071 240 0393

Many of Thorpe Park's attractions and rides are linked with water themes

The 1066 Story

Hastings, East Sussex

The story of the Battle of Hastings and William the Conqueror and the history of Hastings Castle are told in a reconstruction of a medieval siege tent erected within the ruins of Hastings Castle. The audio visual programme with lighting effects lasts for 16 minutes and uses more than 350 slides in a multi-screen presentation narrated by Richard Baker and Sarah Green.

Open every day of the year except for between 4th January and 14th February.

☎ 0424 717963

Thorpe Park

Chertsey, Surrey

A theme park with many of its attractions and rides linked with water themes, Thorpe Park covers approximately 500 acres and half of this is lakes and streams. The white knuckle rides include the Thunder River wild water ride and the Canada Creek log flume ride. There are a wide range of attractions including Model World, a garden containing scale models of most of the world's most famous buildings including the Taj Mahal and the Statue of Liberty. The complex also includes Thorpe Farm, a place of rural quiet with farm buildings and animals grouped around the duck pond. There are water buses and land trains to move about on and an wide range of refreshments in European Square. There are also shops and a craft centre.

Open every day from early April until the end of October.

☎ 0932 562633

THE REGION AT PLAY

Tower Bridge

The City, London EC3
⊖ Tower Hill

Tower Bridge is probably the world's best known bridge, the bridge was opened in 1894 and a new themed presentation opens at the bridge in August 1993 as part of the forthcoming centenary celebrations. The Celebration Story will use audio-animatronic figures to recreate the day the bridge opened, explain how and why it was built and show you what the riverbanks looked like on the day it opened before showing you how the river skyline has changed in 100 years. There is a shop and a restaurant.

Closed until 2nd August 1993 and then open every day.

☎ 071 403 3761

Tower Hill Pageant

Tower Hill, London EC3
⊖ Tower Hill

Developed in association with the Museum of London the Tower Hill Pageant is a "time travel" ride through the history of the City of London and the Tower of London with recreations of moments in the life of the great and the ordinary citizens from Roman times to the present day. There is a shop and there are restaurants nearby.

Open every day except Christmas Day.

☎ 071 709 0081

Treasure Island

Eastbourne, East Sussex

An adventure playground themed on the Treasure Island story. There is galleon and figures and models from the novel as well as a wide range of rides and attractions. There is a gift shop, a cafe and a picnic site.

Open every day between April and October.

☎ 0323 411077

Whitbread Hop Farm

Near Paddock Wood, Kent

The Whitbread Hop Farm is centred around the largest collection of Victorian oast houses in the world. The Hop Story Exhibition recreates the world of hopping and the life of a hop picker during the farm's heyday. Other attractions include the Animal Village, the Birds of Prey collection and the Pottery. The farm is also the home of the Whitbread Shire Horse Centre and there are daily demonstrations of grooming, harnessing and driving as well as displays of drays and harnesses. There is also a woodland nature trail. There are gift shops, a restaurant and picnic areas. There are special events, car rallies, hot air ballooning and open air concerts throughout the year.

Open every day except for Christmas Day, Boxing Day and New Years Day.

☎ 0622 872068

White Cliffs Experience

Dover, Kent

The combined use of actors and high technology special effects tell the story of Dover, recognised for centuries as the Key to England, from the Roman invasion to World War Two. The reconstructions range from a Roman quayside to a street scene during an air raid. There is an adventure playground and a special display for children. There is a restaurant and a gift shop.

Open every day except for Christmas Day.

☎ 0304 214566

Tower Hill Pageant

A London events diary ....

Because the nation's capital is within the London and the South East area the region offers many spectacular attractions in addition to the the wide range of locations that form the main "What to see" listing.

One of the most interesting of these for a visitor to the capital is the Changing of the Guards at Buckingham Palace. From viewpoints outside the railings at the front of the Palace and around the Queen Victoria Memorial it is possible to witness a small part of the pomp and tradition surrounding the Monarchy.

Changing the Guard happens at 11.30 a.m. every day during Spring and Summer, weather permitting, and on alternate days through the rest of the year.

Some of the most spectacular annual events in London happen during the following months, if you want to watch you are advised to find a vantage point early:

January - The Lord Mayor of Westminster's New Years Day Parade - Marching bands around the Westminster area - from 12 noon on the 1st.

January/February - Chinese New Year - lions, dragons and fortune cookies in and around Gerrard Street in London's Chinatown - the day varies depending when Chinese New Year falls.

March - The Oxford and Cambridge Boat Race - the annual challenge between Britain's two oldest universities takes place on the River Thames between Putney and Mortlake - normally on the third Saturday of the month, the time varies with the tide.

Easter - The Easter Show in Battersea Park - not as spectacular as it used to be but still worth a visit - from 12 noon on Easter Sunday.

April - The London Marathon - a 26 mile course from Greenwich through Docklands, the City and Westminster finishing on Westminster Bridge - normally on the third Sunday of the month.

May - The Chelsea Flower Show - one of the world's great displays of flowers and garden design in the grounds of the Royal Hospital at Chelsea - the last week in May.

June - Trooping the Colour - the celebration of the Queen's Official Birthday at which the sovereign reviews the troops in Horse Guards Parade - at 11.00 a.m. on the second Saturday.

November - The Lord Mayor's Show - a street pageant and procession to mark the inauguration of the new Lord Mayor of the City of London - on the second Saturday of the month.

November - Remembrance Day - whilst the commemoration of the dead from World Wars One and Two is something that happens across the country the service at the Cenotaph in Whitehall is the most moving - 11.00 a.m. on the second Sunday of the month.

December - New Years Eve Celebrations - around the fountains and Christmas Tree in Trafalgar Square - all night and most of the morning after on the 31st.

Family days out in *London and the South East*

Nowadays almost all reasonably sized leisure attractions offer facilities and special activities for children and family groups. These can range from an activity playground or special children's trail in a park or garden to reduced price family tickets and special children's sections in large theme parks.

Some attractions are specifically intended for children and families or offer additional activities during school holidays. Amongst the attractions listed in the main London and South East listing the following are particularly intended for family entertainment.

1

1. **Bentley Wildfowl and Motor Museum**
2. **Smugglers Adventure**
3. **Brighton Sea-Life**
4. **London Toy and Model Museum**

2

3

4

Arundel Toy and Military Museum

Arundel, West Sussex

A must for children of all ages. Set in a Georgian cottage in the heart of Arundel is a delightful museum full of dolls, teddy bears, toy soldiers, dolls' houses, military models and toy farms and boats.

Open every weekend, Bank Holidays and every day between the middle of June and the middle of September.

☎ 0903 882908

Badsell Park Farm

Matfield, near Tonbridge, Kent

Badsell Park Farm has a new mountain biking course and organises special Magic Shows every Thursday. There are also special children's events throughout the Summer and Bonfire Night and Christmas Parties. The changing activities on this working arable farm through the growing and harvesting and picking seasons can be observed. There is a farm trail and a woodland and meadow nature trail. There is also a pets and farm animals corner, a gift shop, picnic sites and a cafe. During the season there are "pick your own" facilities.

Open every day between the end of March and the end of November and in December for the Christmas Party.

☎ 0892 832549

Bentley Wildfowl and Motor Museum

Bentley, near Lewes, East Sussex

The museum has a children's education centre offering both "hands-on" fun courses and more educationally testing courses on wildfowl. It is the home of the largest private collection of wildfowl in Britain with species of birds from around the world many of which are tame enough to be fed by hand. Bentley House also contains the Philip Rickman Collection of Wildfowl Paintings and is the home of a museum of roadworthy vintage cars. On Sundays there is a miniature steam railway in the grounds. There is a gift shop, a tea room and a picnic site.

Open every day between the middle of March and early September, the grounds only are also open at weekends except for during January.

☎ 0825 840573

Arundel Toy and Military Museum

Birdland

Near Farnham, Surrey

Birdland has special events and fun days for children throughout the year including a Teddy Bears' Picnic and a Mad Hatter's Tea Party and over Christmas one of the gift shops is converted into Santa's Workshop. Birdland's 20 acres house displays of more than 1,000 birds including many exotic species such as flamingos, toucans and emus, the lake encloses a penguin island. Birdland also features Underwaterworld, an aquarium holding an interesting range of exotic fish. There are gift shops, a cafe and snack bar and a picnic area.

Open every day except for Christmas Day.

☎ 0420 22140

Blean Bird Park

Blean, near Canterbury, Kent

There is a special children's area at Blean with a pets corner. The park is the home of one of the country's largest breeding collections of macaws as well as flocks of cockatoos, parrots and pheasants. There is a children's play area with an adventure playground and a woodland walk. There is a cafe, a tea room and a picnic site as well as a shop.

Open every day except Christmas and Boxing Days.

☎ 0227 471666

Bluebell Railway
Sheffield Park, near Uckfield, East Sussex

During December the Bluebell Railway organises regular "Santa Special" trains every weekend. It is a 7 1/2 mile preserved steam railway line running from Sheffield Park to Horsted Keynes and Newcombe Bridge. The line reopened in 1960 after it was rescued by enthusiasts. The steam locomotives on the line were built between the 1860s and the 1950s and are the largest collection of working locomotives in the south east of England. Sheffield Park Station has been restored to its appearance in the 1880s and includes a museum, shops and a restaurant. Horsted Keynes Station has been refurbished in a 1930s style and has a bar and bookstall. The locomotives' rolling stock includes Pullman restaurant cars.

Open on Sundays all year, Saturdays between March and December and every day from late May until the end of September.

☎ 082572 2370

Borde Hill Garden
Borde Hill, near Haywards Heath, West Sussex

From April until the end of the school Summer holidays Borde Hill organises trout fishing for children and has special events including firework displays. The garden features both formal gardens with rare plants and parkland and woodland estates. It has been planted and cared for over the last one hundred years. It is famous for its camellias and rhododendrons but also contains many unusually species including plants from Burma and China. There are walks through the woodlands. There is a children's adventure playground, a gift shop and a plant centre. There are also restaurants and picnic sites.

Open every day between April and early October and on Sundays in March and October.

☎ 0444 450326

Brambles Wildlife and Rare Breeds
Near Herne, Kent

Animals ranging from rabbits to wallabies and wild cats live in nearly 30 acres of park and woodland. There are also aviaries and a collection of English rare breeds. There is children's playground with a special play area for the under-5s and a shop as well as a tea room and a picnic area.

Open every day from April to the end of October.

☎ 0227 712379

Brighton Sealife Centre
Brighton, East Sussex

Children visiting the Sealife Centre can buy special fish scratch cards; find the fish, scratch off its illustration on the card and answer the question revealed underneath. There are guide books designed to cover three different age levels in the National Curriculum and colouring books for very young children. There is also an indoor play area. The Centre has more than 30 separate aquatic displays including a shark display with an underwater tunnel as a viewing platform. There is a gift shop and a coffee shop.

Open every day except for Christmas Day.

☎ 0273 604234

Buckleys Yesterday's World
Battle, East Sussex

Buckleys has Punch and Judy Shows and clowns on Sundays during the Summer and organises special children's events including Easter Egg Hunts. There is a special Children's Play Village and working model fairground. Housed in Wealden Hall House in the centre of Battle, Buckleys recreates a wide range of everyday scenes from 1850 to 1950. Individual room represent a chemist's shop, a grocers, a sweet shop, a Victorian kitchen, a photographer's studio and a nursery. There is also a reconstructed 1930s railway station. The garden terrace invites you to enjoy a cream tea whilst looking over a typical English Country Garden. There is a shop and a picnic site.

Open every day except Christmas Day and New Years Day.

☎ 0424 775378

Canterbury Tales
Canterbury, Kent

Canterbury Tales offers children juggling lessons and fancy dress in medieval costumes. It is a "state of the art" audio visual presentation of the 14th century pilgrims' journey from London's Tabard Inn to Becket's Tomb in Canterbury Cathedral with vivid presentations of Chaucer's Tales. The exhibition is built within medieval St. Margaret's Church and includes a shop and coffee shop.

Open every day except Christmas Day.

☎ 0227 454888

Carr Taylor Vineyard
Westfield, near Hastings, East Sussex

Although the vineyard is primarily intended for adults it does look after the children of visiting families by providing them with fun activity worksheets showing them what to look out for around the vineyard and special crossword puzzles to keep them occupied. Carr Taylor produces award winning sparkling and and still white wines. Set on south-facing downland slopes the estate also contains bluebell woods. There is a shop.

Open every day between April and Christmas Eve and all weekends between January and April.

☎ 0424 752501

Buckleys Yesterday's World recreate a wide range of everyday scenes from 1850 to 1950.

Chessington World of Adventure

Chessington World of Adventures

Chessington, Surrey

Everything at Chessington is designed for maximum fun for all the family and there are special events throughout the season. The theme park at Chessington was created in 1987 by transforming the site of Chessington Zoo into a series of nine themed entertainment areas. The nine are Transylvania, The Mystic East, Calamity Canyon, English Market Square, The 5th Dimension, Smugglers Cove, Toytown, Circus World and Animal Areas. The are a wide range of white knuckle rides including the Vampire and the Runaway Train and many other attractions and entertainments. The Animal Areas are the redesigned home of the original Chessington Zoo and the animal collections play an active role in the breeding of endangered species. There are shops and restaurants throughout the complex.

Chessington World of Adventures is open every day between the end of March and the end of October, the Animal Areas Zoo is open every day except for between 24th December and 1st January.

☎ 0372 727227

Children's World and Farm

Beckley, near Rye, East Sussex

As its name implies this 600 acre working dairy and hop farm has been especially designed to introduce children to the world of farms and farming. There is a farm trail leading you around the farm's animals, milking and feeding sessions and a working blacksmith to watch. There is a children's theatre and an adventure playground as well as a trekking centre and a grass carting track. The shop sells farm produce, craft goods and antiques. There is a tea room and a picnic site.

Open every day between April and September and at weekends in March.

☎ 0797 260250

Dover Castle

Dover, Kent

There are special events organised at Dover Castle during weekends throughout the Summer including jousting, archery and music. Dover Castle dominates the town and coastal approaches from its position on top of the White Cliffs. Started by the Normans, it is the largest castle in Britain and was the first concentric castle. There are displays throughout the castle including one on the history of the British Army and a model of the Battle of Waterloo. Hellfire Corner is a tour of the underground chambers and tunnels that formed the wartime forward command post during the Second World War. There is a restaurant and a shop.

Closed on Christmas, Boxing and New Years Days.

☎ 0304 201628

Dover Castle

Drusillas Park

Drusillas Park

Near Alfriston, East Sussex

Drusillas Park was founded over 60 years ago as a tea room and today offers a wide range of attractions for children and the whole family. There are special events throughout the Summer months including talent shows, beauty contests and fancy dress competitions. There is live music every day during school holidays. There is a zoo with an interesting and varied collection of wild animals and birds in landscaped, modern, large enclosures and the keepers encourage children to help them feed the animals. There is also a farmyard with friendly animals and "Mildred" a life size model cow that can be milked. The craft workshops in Drusillas Village including a pottery and The Whackey Paint Shop where visitors can screen print their own designs on to T shirts. There is also a miniature railway and a huge adventure playground. Drusillas has eight shops selling a wide range of gifts and souvenirs, a pub, a restaurant, a snack bar and a picnic site.

Open every day except for Christmas and Boxing Days.

☎ 0323 870234

Ethnic Doll and Toy Museum

Whitstable, Kent

The Ethnic Doll and Toy Museum features 100s of authentic dolls from around the world and there are special children's quiz sheets on the dolls. It is based in Whitstable Castle's gatehouse and other displays include dolls' houses ranging from a Teddy Bears' Cottage to a 27 room London town house and teddy bears. There is a working model railway, a shop and a cafe.

Open every day from the end of January to 22nd December.

☎ 0227 771456

Eurotunnel Exhibition Centre

Cheriton, near Folkestone, Kent

Eurotunnel's displays include "hands-on" exhibits and video presentations designed to hold the attention of adults and children alike. The centre is sited close to the UK terminus of the Channel Tunnel. It tells the story of the tunnel's construction, explains about its strategic importancein the European transport grid and enables visitors to simulate what an actual journey through the tunnel will be like. There is also a large N-gauge model railway of the terminal and an observation tower. There is a shop and a picnic site and the centre's cafe is, naturally, french-style.

Open every day except for non-Bank Holiday Mondays between the middle of October and the end of March.

☎ 0303 270111

Fort Fun and Rocky's Adventure Land

Eastbourne, East Sussex

A 2 acre fun park designed especially for the under-12s, Fort Fun has a wide range of exciting rides and attractions. Rocky's Adventure Land is a new extension especially created for the under-5s and is an enchanting yet totally safe area for the young adventurer. There is a cafe and a picnic area.

Rocky's Adventure World is open every day except Christmas and Boxing Days, Fort Fun is open over Easter, at weekends from April to the end of October and every day from July until the middle of September.

☎ 0323 642833

Fort Luton Museum

Chatham, Kent

A Victorian fort that has been restored and now houses a museum and a model railway. The 4 1/2 acres of grounds contain an adventure playground, a pets corner and a collection of "silly sculptures" as well as gardens. There is a craft shop, a cafe and a picnic site.

Open every day from March until Christmas Eve.

☎ 0634 813969

Gatwick Zoo

Charlwood, near Crawley, Surrey

Gatwick Zoo organises special events for children throughout the Summer including "Meet the Animals", juggling and balloon modelling. There are also performing clowns strolling around the grounds. The zoo's 10 acres of landscaped grounds contain a varied display of animals and birds many of which have been successfully bred at the zoo. Monkey Island houses the zoo's breeding troop of squirrel monkeys. The aviary is a walk-through free-flight enclosure about 80 feet long with many exotic species including macaws. There is also a free-flight butterfly house which is temperature controlled to resemble jungle conditions and houses many species of tropical butterflies. There is a gift shop, a cafe and a picnic area.

Open every day except for Christmas and Boxing Days.

☎ 0293 862312

Guinness World of Records

The Trocadero, Coventry Street, London W1
⊖ Piccadilly Circus

The Guinness World of Records is a presentation of some of the most impressive and most visual records from the Guinness Book of Records using life sized models, videos, multi screen audiovisuals and high tech effects. During school holidays special "Beat the record" challenges are organised for children. There is also a shop.

Open every day except Christmas Day.

☎ 071 439 7331

Historic Dockyard

Chatham, Kent

The Historic Dockyard exhibitions are designed to appeal to the whole family and are very visual. Chatham Royal Dockyard was founded by Henry VIII in 1547 and began building ships for the Royal Navy in 1586 with the launching of the Sunne. It constructed more than 400 vessels including Nelson's Victory and the last ship to be built in Chatham was the submarine Ocelot, launched in 1962. The 80 acre site is the most completely preserved Georgian dockyard in the world. The buildings and exhibits around the dockyard tell the story of life in the dockyard from the Commissioner and his officers to the everyday dockyard workers. There are seven major attractions including a 1/4 mile long working ropery. There is a shop and a cafeteria, a tea shop in Summer and picnic sites. There are special events throughout the year.

Open on Wednesdays, Saturdays and Sundays between the end of October and the end of March and every day for the rest of the year except for Tuesdays and non-Bank Holiday Mondays.

☎ 0634 812551

HMS Belfast

Tooley Street, London SE1
⊖ London Bridge

HMS Belfast organises special days when children can come on board, dress up and pretend to be at sea. It is also used as a venue for children's parties and offers educational facilities for projects. It is a Royal Navy cruiser that was built in 1936 and is the largest preserved warship in Europe. It is permanently moored on the south bank of the Thames across the river from the Tower of London. The ship is administered by the Imperial War Museum and visitors can inspect the engine rooms, the control room, the mess decks, the gun turrets and the bridge. There is a shop and a cafe.

Open every day except Christmas Day.

☎ 071 407 6434

Howletts Zoo Park

Bekesbourne, near Canterbury, Kent

Howletts has a special children's club called Zoom and organises events including puppet shows and face painting. There are also special children's quizzes based on the zoo park's collections. Howletts was opened by John Aspinall in 1975 to display his collection of rare breeds from around the world. From the start he intended it to be an important breeding centre and today it has one of the largest collections of tigers in the world and one of the largest of breeding gorillas. It was also the first zoo in this country to breed African elephants successfully.

Open every day except Christmas Day.

☎ 0227 721286

Kent and East Sussex Steam Railway

Tenterden, Kent

There are special children's events and days throughout the year including Postman Pat weekends and Thomas the Tank Engine weekends as well as Christmastime Santa trains. The single track line runs for 7 miles from Tenterden to Northiam with stops at Rolvenden and Wittershaw Road. The 16 steam locomotives date from 1876 onwards and the rolling stock includes the Victorian Train and the London and North Western Railway Director's Saloon. Tenterden Station has been refurbished in Edwardian style and features a display area, museum, gift shop and buffet. The trains carry restaurant cars on Saturday evenings and Sunday lunchtimes during the Summer and there is a tea room at Northiam and picnic sites at both ends of the line.

The line is working every Sunday except during January, on Saturdays from April until early

November and every day from June until the end of September.

☎ 0580 765155

London Dungeon

Tooley Street, London SE1
⊖ London Bridge

Britain's only horror themed adventure depicting torture, death and superstition. The high tech effects make everything shockingly realistic and it is definitely not for young, impressionable children or the weak hearted but most children [and adults] find it irresistible. The life size reconstructions of executions and executions are very impressive. The latest addition is a recreation of the Victorian East End of Jack the Ripper. There is a shop and a cafe.

Open every day.

☎ 071 403 0606

London Planetarium

Marylebone Road, London NW1
⊖ Baker Street

The London Planetarium has been fascinating and mystifying children for generations, it still offers observation of the planets and stars via projection onto the inside of the dome but nowadays the computerised high tech Starburst shows, which last for 30 minutes, are preceded by Space Trail, a new lift off zone with interactive video monitors featuring live satellite communication before you "reach" the observation platform for Starburst.

Open every day except for Christmas Day.

☎ 071 486 1121

London Toy and Model Museum

Craven Hill, London W2
⊖ Paddington

As with all toy museums this is a must for all those who are young or young at heart. There is an impressive display of more than 7,000 commercially made toys and models ranging from an ancient Roman gladiator doll to a modern toy robot. Displays include teddy bears, dolls and dolls' houses as well as model trains, Dinky cars, Meccano kits and model soldiers. The gardens house a miniature railway, a vintage roundabout and a model double decker bus. There is a shop and a cafe and there are special events throughout the Summer.

Open every day.

☎ 071 262 9450

London Zoo

Regent's Park, London NW1
⊖ Camden Town

London Zoo's children's zoo has been entertaining and educating the nation's children for many generations. The Zoological Society of London was founded in 1826 as the world's first public zoo. Although currently the centre of much controversy over its financing and future role in the changing world of animal conservation and care it is still a major attraction with thousands of animals. There is a shop and there are cafes.

Open every day except Christmas Day.

☎ 071 722 3333

Madame Tussaud's

Marylebone Road, London NW1
⊖ Baker Street

Madame Tussaud's is one of London's finest attractions for the whole family. It is the world's largest waxworks and has been established since 1833 and based in the present buildings since 1884. Alongside the traditional galleries of the famous and the infamous there are now many specially created tableaux and an exciting new history of London. The Spirit of London opens for the first time in Spring 1993 and has cost over £10 million. It is a "time taxi" ride through London experiencing the sights, sounds and smells of the great moments of London history using wax figures, audio-animatronic figures and high tech computers. The journey takes you through 400 years from Elizabethan London to the present day. There is a shop and a cafe.

Open every day except Christmas Day.

☎ 071 935 6861

Madame Tussaud's

National Maritime Museum
Romney Road, Greenwich,
London SE10

The National Maritime Museum is a fascinating museum for children and there are always special events and displays during the Summer school holidays. The museum tells the history of the role of the sea and seafaring in the life of the nation. There are large displays of ships, ship models, weapons, uniforms, figureheads, globes, telescopes and marine paintings. There are special sections on two of Britain's best known sailors, Nelson and Cook. The grounds of the museum also house Inigo Jones' Queen's House and the Old Royal Observatory with its museum of astronomy and time. There is a shop and a cafe.

Open every day except for Good Friday, Christmas Day, Boxing Day and New Years Day.

☎ 081 858 4422

Natural History Museum
Cromwell Road, London SW7
⊖ South Kensington

Most children find the Natural History Museum's displays irresistible, especially as they include skeletons of dinosaurs and full-size models of whales. The collection was started as part of Sir Hans Sloane's bequest that created the British Museum but the natural history section was separated in the 1880s to form its own museum. The museum's displays cover all aspects of natural history including geology, evolution and ecology. There is a shop and a restaurant.

Open every day except for Good Friday, over the Christmas period and New Years Day.

☎ 071 938 9123

Palace Pier
Brighton, East Sussex

The seaside pier represents many people's view of what a family seaside resort should be like and Brighton's Palace Pier, built in 1899, is the most popular seaside pier in the country. There is plenty to see and do along its length including rides, dodgems and amusement arcades or you can just stretch out in a deckchair, take the sun and watch the world go by. There are fast food outlets and bars and, in restored full Victorian splendour, the Palm Court Fish Restaurant. During the Summer season there are marching bands, comedy shows and illusionists.

Open every day.

☎ 0273 609361

Port Lympne Zoo
Park Lympne, near Hythe, Kent

Port Lympne is the sister park to Howletts Zoo Park and shares the same children's club, Zoom, and organises special events and competitions. The 300 acres of landscaped park contain a series of open reserves housing herds of rare breeds ranging from deer and antelope to rhinoceroses and elephants. There is a visitor centre, a shop selling gifts and craft goods, a restaurant and picnic areas.

Open every day except for Christmas Day.

☎ 0303 264646

Rare Farm Animals of Hollanden
Hildenborough, near Sevenoaks,
Kent

The farm helps children to understand animals and the countryside by allowing them to work with the farm animals including milking the goats, grooming the ponies and feeding the lambs. It is a sanctuary for rare breeds of a range of British farm animals including horses, cattle, sheep, goats and pigs. It also looks after rare breeds of chickens and a variety of waterfowl. There is a tractor and trailer tour of the farm as well as a woodland and water trail, an adventure playground and a farm shop. There is also a tea room and a picnic site.

Open every day from the end of March until early October.

☎ 0732 832276

Rock Circus
Piccadilly Circus, London W1
⊖ Piccadilly Circus

Because of its subject matter Rock Circus is a fascinating attraction for children as soon as they have started to listen to music. It is a rock and pop themed entertainment creating using wax models and audio-animatronic figures and the technological know-how of the experts from Madame Tussaud's. There are more than 50 figures recreating the story and music of rock and pop from the 1950s to the 1990s and ranging from Bill Haley, Little Richard and Elvis to Madonna and Bono. As well as the fixed displays the revolving stage presents four sets of different groups of stars introduced by Tim Rice's commentary. There is a shop and a cafe.

Open every day.

☎ 071 734 7203

Rock Circus

Rock Circus

Shipwreck Heritage Centre

Hastings, East Sussex

Christopher Lee's narration of the story brings alive this modern "sound and light" show set on a medieval ship in a simulated dock and telling the story of a shipwreck that happened 500 years ago. There are special quiz sheets for children. There are also displays on "Roman and Later Treasures from Shipwrecks". There is a gift shop.

Open every day from Easter until the end of September.

☎ 0424 437452

South of England Rare Breeds Centre

Woodchurch, near Ashford, Kent

The Centre looks after around 500 animals and includes a farm animal corner specially for children where there are tame cattle, pigs and sheep to be looked after. It is a working farm with more than 60 different species of rare farm animals. There is a nature trail, a farm trail and a woodland trail. There is a gift and farm shop, a restaurant and a picnic area. There are fun days for the family and other special events throughout the Summer.

Open every day except for Christmas Day.

☎ 0233 861494

Smart's Amusement Park

Littlehampton, West Sussex

A long-established South Coast entertainments complex with rides and attractions for all the family including rollercoasters, dodgems and funfair rides. There is also a gift shop, a cafe and a picnic site.

Open every day from April until the end of September.

☎ 0903 721200

Tower Hill Pageant

Smugglers Adventure

St. Clements Caves, Hastings, East Sussex

Most children love stories about smugglers and a story set in a cave complex that was actually used as a smugglers' haunt is irresistible. The caves cover 1½ acres, were used by real smugglers in the 18th century and have had wide and varied uses over the last 200 years including as a military hospital, a ballroom, an air raid shelter, a wax works and a jazz club. In 1989 they reopened as a state-of-the-art exhibition of the history of smuggling with more than 50 life size figures, automated models and sound and light effects. The ballroom has also been restored to the way it would have appeared in the 1820s and there is a display on the history of the caves. There is a shop.

Open every day except for Christmas Day.

☎ 0424 422964

Sussex Toy and Model Museum

Brighton, East Sussex

Housed in the arches underneath Brighton railway station is a delightful museum with collections of toy and model soldiers, dolls, cars, trains and planes. There is a tea room and a shop.

Open every day except for non-Bank Holiday Mondays.

Thorpe Park

Chertsey, Surrey

A day at Thorpe Park on a family ticket offers thrills and enjoyment to people of all ages. Thorpe Park covers approximately 500 acres and half of this is lakes and streams. The white knuckle rides include the Thunder River wild water ride and the Canada Creek log flume ride. There are a wide range of attractions including Model World, a garden containing scale models of most of the world's most famous buildings including the Taj Mahal and the Statue of Liberty. The complex also includes Thorpe Farm, a place of rural quiet with farm buildings and animals grouped around the duck pond. There are water buses and land trains to move about on and an wide range of refreshments in European Square. There are also shops and a craft centre.

Open every day from early April until the end of October.

☎ 0932 562633

Tower Hill Pageant

Tower Hill, London EC3
⊖ Tower Hill

Developed in association with the Museum of London the Tower Hill Pageant is a "time travel" ride through the history of the City of

London and the Tower of London with recreations of moments in the life of the great and the ordinary citizens from Roman times to the present day. There is a shop and there are restaurants nearby.

Open every day except Christmas Day.

☎ 071 709 0081

Tower of London

Tower Hill, London EC3
⊖ Tower Hill

Children and castles have a natural affinity and the Tower of London offers more attractions than any other castle. It is one of the most famous and most photographed castles in the world and over the centuries it has been a royal palace, prison, zoo and place of execution. Today it is one of the most visited tourist attractions in the country and the home of the Crown Jewels, the Beefeaters, Traitors' Gate and the famous Ravens. There is a shop.

Open every day.

☎ 071 709 0765

Toy and Model Museum

Lamberhurst, Kent

An oast house has been converted into a museum featuring dolls and teddy bears. There is a special section on Rupert the Bear as well as displays of model cars, a model fairground and a model railway. The complex also includes a village street with period shops and a craft centre. There is a tea room and a picnic site.

Open every day except for Christmas Day.

☎ 0892 890711

Treasure Island

Eastbourne, East Sussex

An adventure playground themed on the Treasure Island story with a special toddlers' area for under-4s and an outdoor play area for under-12s. There is a galleon and figures and models from the novel as well as a wide range of rides and attractions. There is a gift shop, a cafe and a picnic site.

Open every day between April and October.

☎ 0323 411077

Whitbread Hop Farm

Near Paddock Wood, Kent

The Whitbread Hop Farm is centred around the largest collection of Victorian oast houses in the world. The Hop Story Exhibition recreates the world of hopping and the life of a hop picker during the farm's heyday. Other attractions include the Animal Village, the Birds of Prey collection and the Pottery. The farm is also the home of the Whitbread Shire Horse Centre and there are daily demonstrations of grooming, harnessing and driving as well as displays of drays and harnesses. There is also a woodland nature trail. There are gift shops, a restaurant and picnic areas.
There are special events, car rallies, hot air ballooning and open air concerts throughout the year.

Open every day except for Christmas Day, Boxing Day and New Years Day.

☎ 0622 872068

The Whitbread Hop Farm is centred around the largest collection of Victorian oast houses in the world

A scene from the White Cliffs Experience

White Cliffs Experience
Dover, Kent

The combined use of actors and high technology special effects tell the story of Dover, recognised for centuries as the Key to England, from the Roman invasion to World War Two. The reconstructions range from a Roman quayside to a street scene during an air raid. There is an adventure playground and a special display for children. There is a restaurant and a gift shop.

Open every day except for Christmas Day.

☎ 0304 214566

Wilderness Wood
Hadlow Down, near Uckfield, East Sussex

Wilderness Wood is a working wood covering 61 acres, it provides children with Spotter Sheets of things to look for in the woods and they are encouraged to build camps in the woods. There is an extensive network of paths and rides to follow as well as an organised woodland trail of approximately 3/4 of a mile. During the Spring there is also a bluebell trail and around the wood yard there is a tree trail. There is also a woodland play area with an aerial ropeway, a picnic area with barbecues, a tea shop and a gift shop. You can also purchase a range of goods manufactured from the Wood's timber.

Open every day of the year.

☎ 0825 830509

Wildfowl and Wetlands Centre
Arundel, West Sussex

The Wildfowl and Wetlands Trust owns 60 acres of lakes and water meadows alongside the River Arun below Arundel Castle. These provide a home for more than 1,000 swans, geese, ducks and other wildfowl. There is a viewing gallery overlooking the central lake and seven hides dotted around the grounds as well as gravel pathways through the centre. There is a visitor centre with a cinema and gift shop, a restaurant and a picnic site. There are special events and talks throughout the year.

Open every day except Christmas Day.

☎ 0903 883355

Wilderness Wood